FLAGS

D0033751

FLAGS

ERIC INGLEFIELD

Illustrated by
Tony Mould

Consultants
William G. Crampton M Ed
David J. Lally

PRENTICE HALL PRESS • NEW YORK

Published in 1987 by Prentice Hall Press
A Division of Simon & Schuster, Inc.
Gulf + Western Building
One Gulf + Western Plaza
New York, NY 10023

Originally published in the United Kingdom by Kingfisher Books Limited
Previously published in the United States by Arco Publishing, Inc.

PRENTICE HALL PRESS is a trademark of Simon & Schuster, Inc.

Library of Congress Catalog Card Number: 84-70797
ISBN 0-668-06262-2
Color separations by Newsele Litho, Milan
Printed and bound in Italy by Vallardi Industrie Grafiche, Milan

10 9 8 7 6 5 4 3 2 1

First Prentice Hall Press Edition

CONTENTS

INTRODUCTION

In his graphic account of the battle of Rosebecque in 1382, the 14th-century French historian Jean Froissart records the dramatic arrival on the battlefield of the old red war flag of France, the oriflamme of St Denis. The flag was held in such awe and esteem by the soldiers that its appearance brought them great comfort. This simple incident testifies to the emotional power that can be radiated by a piece of coloured cloth fixed to a pole. One's reaction to a flag is of course a response to the ideas or feelings with which it is associated, for a flag is primarily a symbol, not a mere piece of decoration. For the French troops at Rosebecque the oriflamme was an expression of divine support for their cause.

Flags have had an important role in some of the most momentous events in the history of mankind, inspiring patriotic fervour, reinforcing the joyfulness of a celebration or expressing the solemn dignity of an occasion of mourning. The power of massed displays of national emblems to impress subject peoples was well understood by the conquering legions of ancient Rome. In modern times, the power of flags is still recognized and used to great effect. Rarely have flags been used to such a powerful propaganda effect as in the huge and impressive parades seen in Nazi Germany in the 1930s or in the Soviet Union and China today.

Because they are symbols, flags may mean different things to different people. When Father Pierre-Jean de Smet, for example, rode out with American cavalry in 1868 to discuss peace with the Sioux Indian leader Sitting Bull, he carried with him a flag portraying the Virgin Mary as a sign of peace. But the symbol was misinterpreted by the Indians who associated flags only with battle and a massacre nearly ensued. Flags thus embody the ideals and historical experience of the people they represent and are important social and historical documents worthy of close study.

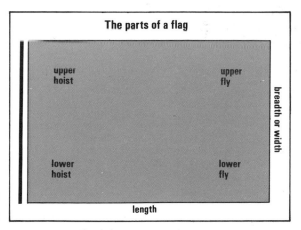

The parts of a flag

upper hoist

upper fly

lower hoist

lower fly

breadth or width

length

Left: Traditional banners are carried by a group of Japanese horsemen as they re-enact an ancient tournament.

Signal flags are used to dress modern warships while in port

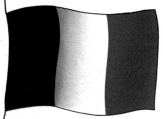

A flag of mourning is flown at half mast to leave space for Death's invisible flag above it.

In some countries the national flag can even be seen as a decoration on everyday things.

Flag Etiquette and Customs

Over the centuries all kinds of customs and ceremonies involving flags have grown up throughout the world. Everywhere flags have emerged as symbols of authority or emblems of patriotism and have been accorded the respect due to them.

Some nations have devised regulations to ensure that their flags are treated with dignity. Republics, in particular, view their emblems with the same awe shown towards royalty by people in monarchies. The United States, for example, has drawn up strict rules to prevent any disrespect to the national flag. In contrast, the United Kingdom shows remarkable tolerance over the display of its flag, which can even be seen decorating shopping bags and tea mugs. Such apparent irreverence would be frowned upon in such countries as Costa Rica, where private citizens are forbidden by law from flying the national flag. Many of these countries have a special state flag for display by government bodies, and a civil flag for use by its citizens.

Care in the treatment of foreign national flags is even more important. Many a diplomatic incident has arisen over some real or imagined slight to the flag. Correct protocol is essential not only in giving equal status to flags of equal importance but also in following correct precedence when flying flags of different rank.

Of the many ceremonies and customs involving flags, there is space here to mention only the most common.

Traditions followed on ships are recognized internationally. On special occasions while in port, for example, ships are dressed, or decorated, overall with flags of the International Code of Signals. The letter 'P' of this code is also used as a signal to indicate that the ship is about to set sail. In a foreign port ships fly the merchant flag of the host country as a symbol of courtesy as well as their own ensign. On the open sea, ships passing a warship generally dip their ensigns in salute.

On land, flags are often seen flying over buildings on national occasions. At times of mourning for an important person they are flown at half-mast, and a national flag is draped over the casket as a mark of respect. Colour flags of the armed services are displayed in impressive military parades, while those no longer in use are ceremonially laid up for preservation in churches. More commonly, flags of all kinds add colour, excitement and interest to countless less formal occasions.

Colours are traditionally presented to military units in impressive ceremonial parades

At football matches supporters often make a dazzling display with flags in their team's colours

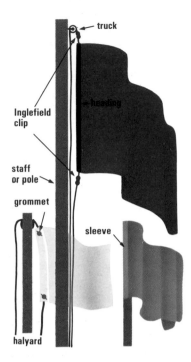

truck

Inglefield clip

staff or pole

grommet

heading

sleeve

halyard

A GLOSSARY OF FLAG TERMS

Armorial banner A flag bearing the design from a shield extended to fit the shape of the flag.

Badge Any emblem added to a flag and which can generally be used separately.

Banner Any kind of flag, especially one with a complex design or coat-of-arms, or a flag hanging from a crossbar.

Banneret A small ceremonial flag decorating bagpipes or a trumpet.

Battle honour An inscription on a military colour or a metal clip on an accompanying streamer devised to show a unit's successes.

Bunting A strong cloth used for flags; also a string of small decorative flags in that material.

Burgee The flag of a yacht club, generally triangular or swallow-tailed (see pages 14, 35).

Canton A rectangular area in the top corner of a flag near the staff.

Charge A symbol or other object on a flag, not normally used separately.

Civil ensign See MERCHANT FLAG.

Civil flag A national flag used by private citizens on land.

Cockade A rosette or bow of national colours sometimes fixed to the top of a flag staff and often worn on hats in the 18th century.

Colour or **Colours** The flag of a military unit, such as a regiment.

Counterchanged Having two colours reversed on either side of a line across a flag or emblem, as in the shield in Swaziland's flag.

Courtesy flag The merchant flag of the host country flown by a visiting foreign ship.

Deface To add a badge or charge to a flag already in existence.

Dexter The right-hand side of a flag from the bearer's viewpoint, or the left side as seen by the viewer.

Dipping Briefly lowering a flag as an expression of courtesy.

Dress ship To decorate a ship with flags on a special occasion.

Emblem A heraldic device or other distinguishing symbol representing a person, country or organization.

Ensign A flag indicating nationality flown by ships at the stern or by government services on land, such as the air force.

Field The background colour of a flag or heraldic shield.

Fimbriation A narrow band of colour separating two other colours.

Finial The ornamental top of a flag staff.

Flag of convenience The flag of a country flown by foreign ships registered there because of its less strict maritime regulations.

Flammule A flag edging shaped like a tongue or flame, often used on oriental flags (see pages 15, 41).

Fly Part of a flag farthest away from the staff and usually occupying that half of its area.

Gonfalon A flag, often with tails, hung from a crossbar (see page 15).

Gonfanon A medieval flag with square tails and flown laterally from a staff (see page 15).

Government flag See STATE FLAG.

Guidon A small, swallow-tailed military flag.

Hoist To raise a flag; also part of a flag nearest the staff, usually occupying that half of its area.

Horsetail A real or artificial horse's tail used as a decoration on vexilloids or oriental military flags.

House flag The flag of a commercial organization.

Jack A small flag of nationality flown at the prow of a ship.

Jolly Roger A black flag with white emblems associated with pirates.

Masthead pennant A long tapering flag used on a warship to show it is on active service.

Merchant flag The flag of nationality flown by merchant ships; also known as the civil ensign.

National flag In this book, the flag used by private citizens of a country (see CIVIL FLAG).

Naval ensign The flag of nationality flown from the stern of a warship.

Obverse The side of a flag seen when the staff is on the viewer's left.

Pennant Generally a small tapering flag used as a rank flag on ships or as a wall souvenir or decoration.

Prayer flag A small flag bearing inscriptions expressing prayers used in oriental countries.

Rank flag A flag indicating a person's status, generally in military forces.

Reverse The side of a flag seen when the staff is on the viewer's right.

Semaphore A system of signalling with two flags held in various positions.

Sinister The left-hand side of a flag from the bearer's viewpoint, or the right side as seen by the viewer.

Standard A flag of various kinds, including: an ancient vexilloid; a long tapering medieval flag bearing a heraldic design; a heraldic military flag; a heraldic royal banner.

State ensign The government flag flown on non-military vessels, such as those used by fisheries or customs.

State flag The government flag flown on land on state property.

Streamer A very long narrow flag, or a ribbon.

Tricolour A flag with three colours, generally arranged in stripes.

Tugh A Mongol vexilloid.

Vane A decorative metal plaque used as a flag on Viking ships.

Vexilloid Any object fulfilling the role of a flag but generally different in appearance, such as a staff with emblems attached to it.

Vexillology The scientific study of all aspects of flags.

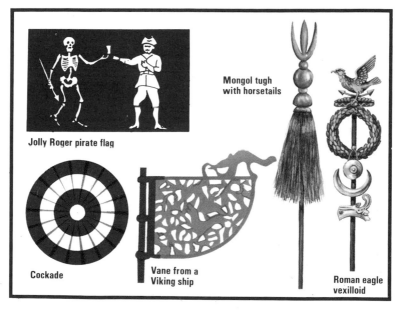

Jolly Roger pirate flag

Mongol tugh with horsetails

Cockade

Vane from a Viking ship

Roman eagle vexilloid

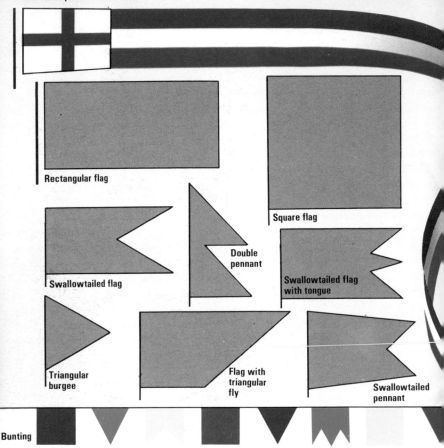

Masthead pennant or streamer

Rectangular flag

Square flag

Double pennant

Swallowtailed flag

Swallowtailed flag with tongue

Triangular burgee

Flag with triangular fly

Swallowtailed pennant

Bunting

FLAG DESIGN

FLAGS OF ALL SHAPES

When looking at the dazzling array of flags outside the United Nations buildings in New York, it is easy to miss the obvious fact that, with one or two exceptions, all the flags on display are plainly rectangular in shape. Their brilliant colours arranged into all kinds of fascinating designs are enough to make flags objects of great beauty. Variations in shape from a plain rectangle would simply be unnecessary embellishment, although they do exist, as shown at the top of this page.

During the long historical development of flags around the world, however, a rich variety of flag shapes did arise. During the Middle Ages the need for flags to identify individual contingents in military campaigns led to the creation of a wide range of designs and shapes, starting from the simple pennant tied to a knight's lance.

Apart from upright rectangular banners and triangular pennants of various designs, many other shapes, such as those shown above, were created during these early times. Among them were the many-tailed gonfanon, the hanging banner known as a gonfalon, the oriflamme used in France and flown

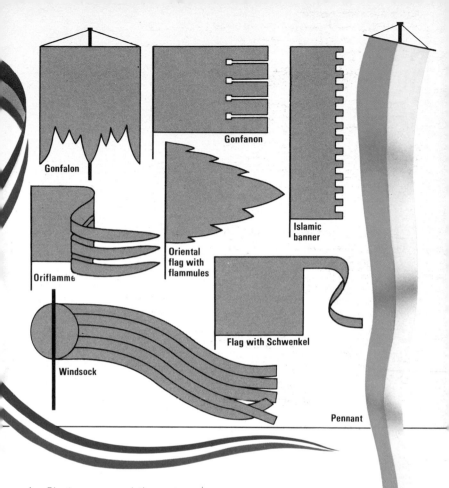

Gonfalon

Gonfanon

Islamic banner

Oriental flag with flammules

Oriflamme

Flag with Schwenkel

Windsock

Pennant

by Charlemagne, and the rectangular banner with a tail called a Schwenkel, which was popular in Germany. At sea the long swallow-tailed streamer was developed for dramatic display at the top of ships' masts.

In the East, flags with even more unusual shapes appeared. The windsock, for example, was a Japanese creation, while a triangular banner with flammules and yak tail decorations was adopted by Genghis Khan.

Such early exotic flags are now only to be seen in history books. Many disappeared as the more practical rectangular flag and its variants became standardized throughout the world.

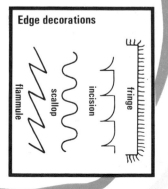

Edge decorations

flammule

scallop

incision

fringe

Two forms of cross make up the design of the Jamaican coastguard flag.

5:9

BASIC PATTERNS IN FLAG DESIGN

Although the shape of modern flags has become generally standardized as a basic rectangle, the patterns of colours used to make up their characteristic designs show a remarkable variety. Within this wealth of pattern, however, certain basic shapes can be detected in flags from all over the world. Apart from the use of an overall colour, the most common pattern consists of stripes, either horizontal or vertical, in various colours.

In addition, more complex patterns are found, some of them deriving from European heraldry, as explained in the following pages. The *canton* is seen, for example, in the American Stars and Stripes flag and in the flags of some former British possessions, such as Australia or New Zealand, where it is used to display the British Union Flag. A *quarterly* design is used for the flag of Panama, while the *triangle* is seen in the flags of Czechoslovakia, Guyana and Jordan. A *serration* divides the colours in Qatar's distinctive flag, and an all-round *border* decorates the flags of Grenada and the Maldive Islands.

Various kinds of *crosses* form the basic design of many flags in parts of the world with a Christian history. The most common are the cross of St George and its variant, the Scandinavian cross; the saltire, or St Andrew's cross; and the Greek cross. The ensign flown by the Jamaican coastguard, shown above, illustrates a combination of two such crosses: a St George's cross, with a saltire occupying the canton.

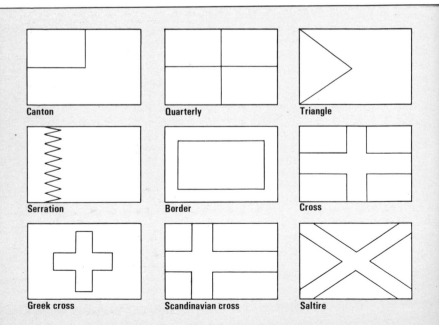

Canton Quarterly Triangle

Serration Border Cross

Greek cross Scandinavian cross Saltire

16

Heraldic shield partitions

The design of many flags seen in the western world today has been influenced by the patterns formed by partitions in heraldic shields.

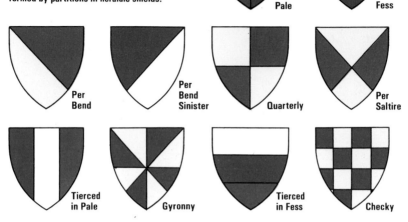

Per Pale

Per Fess

Per Bend

Per Bend Sinister

Quarterly

Per Saltire

Tierced in Pale

Gyronny

Tierced in Fess

Checky

HERALDRY IN FLAG DESIGN

The development of heraldry in medieval Europe created a wide range of distinctive designs for display on the shields and banners of kings and nobles as they rode into battle. The coats-of-arms devised by the court heralds were drawn up according to strict rules and with certain characteristic features. The *partitions* by which they divided up the shield in the coat-of-arms were also found in the corresponding banners they created by extending the shield design to cover the whole area of the banner. An example is the quartered banner of Spain, shown on the right, which was used from the 13th to the 16th century.

Heraldic shield partitions have thus influenced the basic design of many of today's flags, as shown on the facing page. Shields divided *per pale* or *per fess*, or *tierced in pale* or *in fess* have obvious parallels in the stripes of many modern flags. *Quarterly*, *gyronny* and *checky* partitions are also seen in flags with heraldic origins.

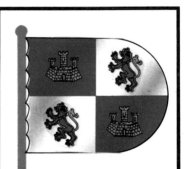

An heraldic banner used in Spain from the 13th to the 16th century has a quarterly design combining the arms of Castile (first and fourth quarters) and León (second and third quarters). In such *canting arms* the objects reveal the names they represent.

Simple charges, or ordinaries

The simple geometric charges
seen on heraldic shields have
helped to create the designs
of many of today's flags. Shapes
representing objects are also
seen.

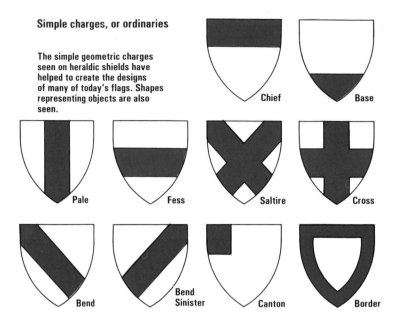

Chief

Base

Pale

Fess

Saltire

Cross

Bend

Bend
Sinister

Canton

Border

The designs of European heraldic shields are divided up not only by the partitions described on the previous page, but also by simple geometric shapes known as *ordinaries* or *simple charges*, which are set upon a background colour called the *field* or *ground*.

More complex charges were also used as symbols to identify individuals. These would be chosen for some personal or family reason and would also appear on the banner derived from the shield design. Examples of such charges are the castle and lion in the Spanish banner on page 17. Other historic charges include the *fleur-de-lis*, the lion rampant and the heraldic eagle illustrated above.

Flags of more recent design often carry charges that are not of heraldic origin. Like early heraldic symbols that came to represent the states ruled by their owners, these modern charges are symbols of whole nations. Examples are the maple leaf of Canada and the straw hat of Lesotho. Crossed swords

are seen on Jordan's army flag, shown on the right.

As well as simple charges, whole coats-of-arms or shields from the arms came to be displayed as *badges* on some European flags after the advent of heraldry. The arms of Portugal and Finland, which appear on their respective state flags, are only two of many examples.

Counterparts of European coats-of-arms also appeared in the East. Medieval Japanese warriors displayed heraldic badges called *mons* on the protective hoods they wore in battle, and these later developed into military banners. The mon often had a circular design incorporating winged insects and flowers. It was the forerunner of the strikingly modern emblems seen on Japanese prefecture flags today (see page 33).

Although not heraldic in origin, the Mongolian *soyonbo* emblem, shown on the right, is another example of a traditional symbol used as a badge on the national flag.

Traditional charges

Fleur-de-lis

Lion rampant

Eagle

Modern charges

Maple leaf, Canada

Straw hat, Lesotho

Swords, Jordanian army

crest

shield

supporter

supporter

compartment

ONE ZAMBIA ONE NATION

scroll with motto

The most complex charges seen on flags
today are complete heraldic coats-of-arms,
or achievements. Around the shield are
additional features that have some symbolical
significance for the owner. Many nations,
as well as individuals and institutions,
have such coats-of-arms or similar emblems.
The heraldic arms of Zambia, above, also
appear on the presidential flag.

Badges

The Portuguese coat-of-arms
appears as a badge on the
national flag. It consists
of a shield charged with other
shields and placed upon an
armillary sphere.

The coat-of-arms of
Finland consists of
a shield alone. On
the national flag
the design appears
in a shield of a
different shape.

The badge on Mongolia's flag
combines the star of Communism
with the traditional soyonbo symbol.
The flame now represents progress;
the sun and moon, eternal life;
the triangles, a warning to enemies;
the bars, honesty and strength;
the Yin-Yang symbol, watchfulness.

19

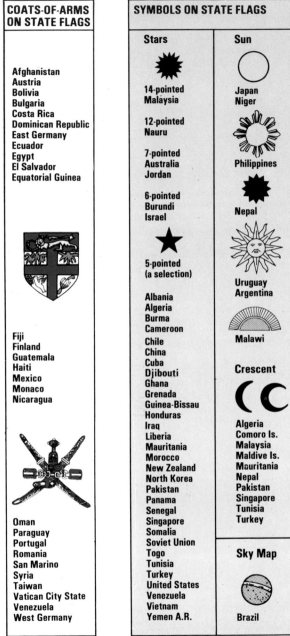

COATS-OF-ARMS ON STATE FLAGS

Afghanistan
Austria
Bolivia
Bulgaria
Costa Rica
Dominican Republic
East Germany
Ecuador
Egypt
El Salvador
Equatorial Guinea

Fiji
Finland
Guatemala
Haiti
Mexico
Monaco
Nicaragua

Oman
Paraguay
Portugal
Romania
San Marino
Syria
Taiwan
Vatican City State
Venezuela
West Germany

SYMBOLS ON STATE FLAGS

Stars

14-pointed
Malaysia

12-pointed
Nauru

7-pointed
Australia
Jordan

6-pointed
Burundi
Israel

5-pointed
(a selection)

Albania
Algeria
Burma
Cameroon
Chile
China
Cuba
Djibouti
Ghana
Grenada
Guinea-Bissau
Honduras
Iraq
Liberia
Mauritania
Morocco
New Zealand
North Korea
Pakistan
Panama
Senegal
Singapore
Somalia
Soviet Union
Togo
Tunisia
Turkey
United States
Venezuela
Vietnam
Yemen A.R.

Sun

Japan
Niger

Philippines

Nepal

Uruguay
Argentina

Malawi

Crescent

Algeria
Comoro Is.
Malaysia
Maldive Is.
Mauritania
Nepal
Pakistan
Singapore
Tunisia
Turkey

Sky Map

Brazil

Animals

Albania
Zambia

Sri Lanka

Anguilla

Bhutan

Papua New Guinea

Uganda

Map

Cyprus

20

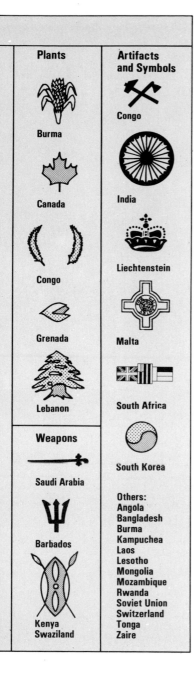

Plants	Artifacts and Symbols
Burma	**Congo**
Canada	**India**
Congo	**Liechtenstein**
Grenada	**Malta**
Lebanon	**South Africa**
Weapons	**South Korea**
Saudi Arabia	**Others:** Angola Bangladesh Burma Kampuchea Laos Lesotho Mongolia Mozambique Rwanda Soviet Union Switzerland Tonga Zaire
Barbados	
Kenya Swaziland	

MODERN EMBLEMS AND SYMBOLS

Many of the world's flags today display charges that have some special significance for the nation as a whole. Heraldic coats-of-arms or shields are to be seen on the flags of various countries around the world, particularly those colonized in the past by European powers. These countries are listed on the opposite page. Among them are former Spanish colonies in South and Central America, such as Peru, whose coats-of-arms appears in the national flag illustrated above.

Other countries have preferred to display simple objects or groups of objects as symbols of national identity. Canada's maple leaf, shown above, is one example. Other common symbols seen in national flags today are listed in the table on the left. Many of these symbols were chosen because they have a special significance for the country concerned, such as the cedar tree of Lebanon or the May Sun of Argentina. Such symbols are often unique to particular countries, such as the *chakra* wheel of India or the nutmeg of Grenada.

Some symbols have a wider significance than purely national emblems. These demonstrate the bonds between nations sharing the same political or religious ideology. The five-pointed star, for instance, is in widespread use on the flags of Communist regimes, while the crescent moon almost invariably identifies a flag as belonging to an Islamic nation.

Fuller explanations of the symbols on individual flags can be found on pages 53–123.

THE MEANINGS OF COLOURS

Although the bright colours used in flags have great decorative appeal, they have rarely been chosen simply because they are beautiful. Particular colours are selected for various reasons – historical, political or symbolical – and each nation has arrived at its choice through its own special circumstances. Explanations of the colours in individual national flags are given on pages 53–123, but some useful generalizations can be made.

Some countries, such as Spain, Sweden and Switzerland, have simply derived the colours in their flags from their heraldic past, without any conscious attempt to select particular colours for their symbolical associations. In the same way, blue, white and red appeared separately in early French flags without any special ideological significance, but after they were combined to form the tricolour of

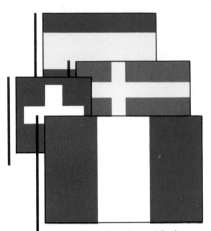

Some flags, such as those of Spain, Sweden, Switzerland and France, use old heraldic or dynastic colours.

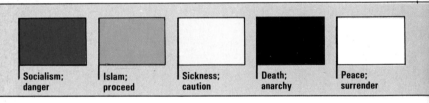

| Socialism; danger | Islam; proceed | Sickness; caution | Death; anarchy | Peace; surrender |

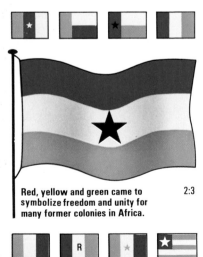

Red, yellow and green came to symbolize freedom and unity for many former colonies in Africa.

2:3

the Revolution of 1789 they came to be regarded as a symbol of liberty throughout the world and inspired the design of many other national flags.

Flags in plain colours have long been given special meanings, as suggested above. Sometimes these colours have been deliberately adopted for national flags because of what they symbolize, particularly the red of revolutionary socialism, the white of peace and the green of Islam.

Colours are also chosen for their more obvious associations. Green is often used to symbolize a nation's forests or agriculture, red the blood shed by its patriots, and so on. In some cases, the colours of one country's flag are taken up by other nations for political reasons. Ghana's red, yellow and green, for example, were adopted as the colours of pan-African liberation by several newly independent nations in the late 1950s and 60s.

FLAGS FOR ALL PURPOSES

Flags are essentially symbols that inspire a sense of unity among people, whether a whole nation or simply a group of individuals forming an association. In the same way, the flags of individual monarchs or national presidents are intended to create a feeling of corporate respect. It is because of their ability to call forth an appropriate emotion that flags can be used in a wide variety of situations. They can add to the great joy of a happy national event, the patriotic fervour of a great military parade, the carefree informality of a country fête, or the awesome solemnity of a state funeral. No special flags are required for any of these occasions. Special flags are created when particular groups of people or institutions require an identifying symbol. Some of these are described on the next few pages.

FLAGS OF HEADS OF STATE

Long before the appearance of the first flags that truly represented ordinary citizens, the flags used to symbolize a nation were the banners of their rulers. For many centuries, the monarch was readily regarded as the embodiment of the state. Louis XIV's famous dictum 'L'état, c'est moi!' (*I am the state*) was merely repeating in a memorable catchphrase the commonly held belief in the divine right of kings to rule. National banners were thus the symbols of royal authority until the advent of truly national flags in the revolutionary atmosphere of the 18th century.

Although their importance as national emblems declined as national flags evolved, the flags of royalty did not entirely disappear. Below are some of the flags used by Queen Elizabeth II. The royal standard is the official banner of the monarch of the United Kingdom, and has a history dating back to Edward III in the 14th century. Special forms of the royal standard are displayed in Commonwealth countries which recognize the Queen as head of state, including Australia, Canada, Jamaica and New Zealand. In Commonwealth countries with republican governments and their own heads of state, the Queen flies her blue personal standard as head of the Commonwealth.

Among the world's other monarchies are Belgium, Denmark and Sweden, which fly royal standards based on the national flag, with the state or royal coat-of-arms in the centre. Like the royal flags of Holland, Norway, Iran, Nepal and Thailand, which incorporate national or royal emblems, the Japanese imperial standard displays the traditional chrysanthemum symbol of the emperor.

Special flags are also used by the leaders of nations with republican forms of government. These generally represent the office of head of state, not the individuals who hold the post for a period of time. However, some slight variations in design may occur. The flag representing the French presidency, for example, has for many years been the national tricolour with the president's initials in the centre. During the presidency of General Charles de Gaulle, however, the double-barred cross of Lorraine was included beneath the initials because of its special role as a symbol of his Free French forces in

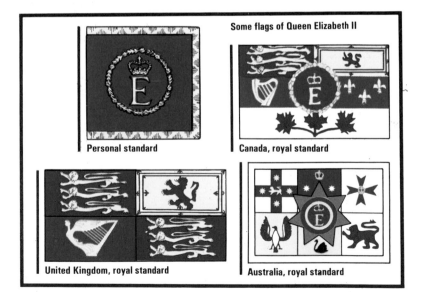

Some flags of Queen Elizabeth II

Personal standard

Canada, royal standard

United Kingdom, royal standard

Australia, royal standard

Sweden, royal flag   1:2

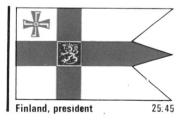
Japan, imperial flag   2:3

United States, president   26:33

West Germany,   1:1
president

Israel, president   1:1

Zambia, president   3:4

Guyana, president   1:1

Gabon, president   1:1

World War II. This oblong flag was superseded by a square one under Georges Pompidou, who had his initials only in the centre. His successor, Giscard d'Estaing introduced a new design – a more oblong version of the tricolour with a gold axe and fasces emblem within a wreath of laurel in the centre. The present President uses a similar tricolour but with his own badge of an oak tree combined with an olive tree in blue in the centre. This symbolizes the unity of France.

Most presidential flags prominently display the state coat-of-arms. Some, such as those of Egypt and Finland, are only slight variations of the national flag, while others, including those of Gabon and Guyana, are specially created designs.

In some countries special flags are also used by heads of government and departmental ministers.

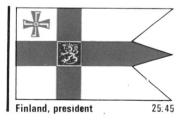
Finland, president   25.45

Egypt, president   2:3

MILITARY FLAGS

One of the earliest uses of flags was as rallying points on the field of battle. Both in the East, where ancient Chinese armies were divided into units, each carrying a different plain-coloured flag, and in Europe, where each Roman legion raised its own distinguishing eagle standard, the importance of symbols which troops could easily identify was recognized.

In the Middle Ages, the development of helmets that completely hid the face of the wearer led to the need for identifying symbols on surcoats, shields and banners. With the growth of heraldry came a welter of brightly coloured banners adopted by kings and nobles and carried by their troops. Into battle alongside these banners went flags portraying favourite patron saints or symbols representing them. The cross of St George, for instance, became the symbol universally adopted by the Christian Crusaders.

During the Reformation and Counter-Reformation, complex allegorical scenes proclaiming the justice of each side's cause appeared on the flags carried by Protestant and Catholic armies. In the following century ornate heraldic designs, flattering the noble

Scottish troops carry their colours into battle in the Crimean War

Distinct from the colours used by individual units are the national military flags flown over army and air force establishments around the world. Other military flags are those used by high-ranking officers. A selection of both types of flag is shown here.

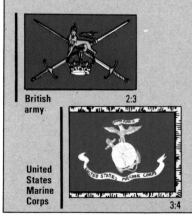

British army   2:3

United States Marine Corps   3:4

patrons of the regiments concerned, were seen on European battlefields. But some means of identifying the nationality of the troops could usually be found on these flags. The English ones, for instance, bore the St George's cross in the canton, while their French counterparts displayed a white cross in the centre.

As time passed, flags representing individual regiments, known as *colours*, came into existence and recorded military victories and honours. These ornate flags also incorporated accessories that included gold fringes, ornamental finials, decorative cords with tassels, and ribbons to which battle honours, orders and decorations were pinned.

In some countries it also became the tradition for military units to have additional colours presented to them by the head of state. These were known as the king's, or queen's, colours or the presidential colours.

Because troops rarely become involved in close hand-to-hand fighting

The great victories won by a regiment are proudly displayed on its colours.

in modern warfare, regimental colours are seldom needed in battle today. But traditional ceremonies associated with them are still continued. One of the best known is the British Trooping the Colour ceremony, when regimental colours are carried past assembled lines of troops so that they can learn to recognize them.

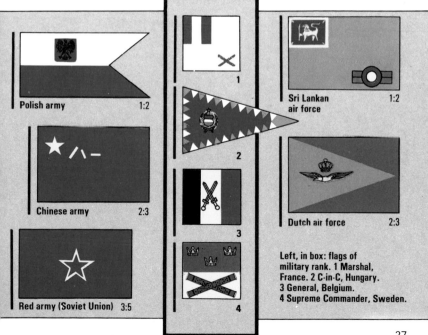

Polish army   1:2

Chinese army   2:3

Red army (Soviet Union)   3:5

Sri Lankan air force   1:2

Dutch air force   2:3

Left, in box: flags of military rank. 1 Marshal, France. 2 C-in-C, Hungary. 3 General, Belgium. 4 Supreme Commander, Sweden.

FLAGS AT SEA

Flags have been used on ships at sea since ancient times. Among the earliest were the fish ensigns displayed with tassels on the prows of ships in the Aegean Sea over 4,000 years ago.

In the Middle Ages, the nationality of ships was indicated by huge emblems painted on the sails and by the shields of knights on board along the gunwales, while the banner of the king or noble in command would be hoisted at the masthead or stern. Trading ships plying across the North Sea often topped their mast with a cross above a streamer in the colours of the home port and perhaps the pennant of the merchant owner. In this way a distinction arose between the flags flown by merchant ships and warships, a tradition that still applies widely today.

From the 16th century, as ships

British merchant flag (Red Ensign) 1:2

British navy ensign (White Ensign) 1:2

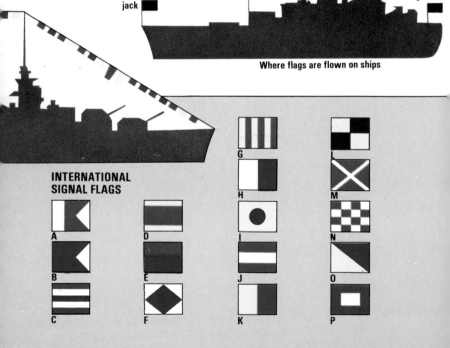

masthead pennant (warship)

house flag (merchant ships)

high-ranking officer on board

jack

ensign

Where flags are flown on ships

INTERNATIONAL SIGNAL FLAGS

A D G L

B E H M

C F I N

J O

K P

ventured farther afield, flags became even more important as a means of establishing ownership and nationality. The *ensign*, flown from the stern, and the *jack*, hoisted at the prow, became the recognized flags of nationality and are still used today. In addition, merchant ships displayed the *house* flag of the owner (now often seen as an emblem on the funnel). As well as the jack and ensign, the *suite of colours* flown by warships included a *masthead pennant*, a long tapering streamer flown at the mainmast. The flags of high-ranking officers are also flown today.

The designs of flags seen on ships today vary greatly from country to country. Most countries use their national (civil) flag as their merchant flag and naval ensign, while others fly their state flag. A large number of countries have a different naval ensign, while a few, such as Israel, use a different merchant flag. Many countries, including the United Kingdom, have different designs for all three flags. Jacks of interesting designs derived from the national flag are also seen, as are flags for use by coastguard and customs services.

As a means of sending messages, signal flags appeared in the 18th century and are still in use.

Japan,
naval ensign   2:3

Italy, jack   1:1

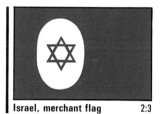

Israel, merchant flag   2:3

Elaborate banners add to the colour of a Buddhist religious procession

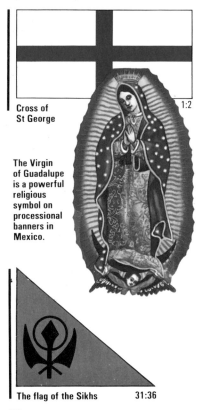

Cross of
St George

1:2

The Virgin
of Guadalupe
is a powerful
religious
symbol on
processional
banners in
Mexico.

The flag of the Sikhs   31:36

RELIGIOUS FLAGS

In ancient times, the standards that soldiers carried into battle were often regarded as sacred symbols personifying their gods. Ancient Egyptian, Greek and Roman armies all believed in the supernatural power radiated by their standards, and to lose one in battle was considered a disaster and a disgrace. There is a close relationship in the religious symbolism of these early standards and the spiritual totems created by other cultural groups throughout the world. This is graphically illustrated by comparing a Roman standard with, for example, a totem pole carved by Indians of northwestern America.

The same religious power was ascribed by the Romans to their first Christian standard, the Labarum of Emperor Constantine (see page 40). In the same way, Christian armies in medieval Europe confidently expected their flags of patron saints to protect them in battle and to ensure them victory. All kinds of religious symbols thus found their way into the design of flags in the western world. The most common has been the Christian cross, while representations of the Virgin Mary have been widely used on banners in Catholic countries. One of these, the Virgin of Guadalupe, played a significant role in the history of Mexico (see page 50).

Elsewhere in the world, other religions developed their own flags. Islamic banners, for example, adopted ornate designs with beautiful calligraphy, and the crescent moon became a universal symbol still seen on the national flags of Islamic countries.

The flag of the Buddhists   2:3

Red flags flutter over a parade celebrating the Russian Revolution

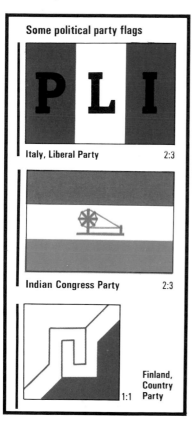

Some political party flags

Italy, Liberal Party   2:3

Indian Congress Party   2:3

Finland, Country Party   1:1

POLITICAL FLAGS

All national flags can be said to be political in that they are symbols of a nation's ideology and way of life. But even within nations, whether tolerated or not by their governments, there are also individuals and groups with their own ideas about the community's needs and the ways these can be satisfied. In truly democratic countries, political parties of all shades of opinion exist and vie with each other for influence. In doing so, they use distinctive flags as unifying symbols to rally support.

Political party flags can be of several types. Some are simple stripes; others are variations of the national flag, such as that of the Italian Liberal Party, which is the national flag with their initials placed on it. Some, such as that of the Indian Congress Party, display a well-known election symbol, the simple spinning wheel popularised by Gandhi.

Completely original designs incorporating special symbols characterize the flags of many other political parties, including that of the Finnish Country Party. More international in spirit are the flags of Communist parties around the world, which are often based on the traditional red flag with the five-pointed star and combinations of various workers' implements, such as the hammer, sickle and hoe.

Political party flags can also influence the design of national flags, as they did in some newly independent countries in Africa.

31

PROVINCIAL AND REGIONAL FLAGS

During the Middle Ages, when the boundaries of European countries were vastly different from those of today, national flags as we know them did not exist. Armies fought under the personal banners of their king, the individual nobles who paid for their services, or the patron saint who would guarantee them victory. Nevertheless, it was at this time that places with a sense of regional identity, including some cities and ports, adopted emblems of their own. Among these were the *cantons*, or provinces, of Switzerland and the great trading ports of the Baltic and Mediterranean.

The emblems used by the provincial authorities took the form of heraldic coats-of-arms and the banners derived

The province of Salzburg, like other Austrian provinces, flies a flag with horizontal stripes in the colours of its medieval arms. Red and white are the Austrian national colours.

Flags with heraldic and more recent emblems

Hordaland, Norway

Brabant, Belgium

Glarus, Switzerland

Friesland, Netherlands

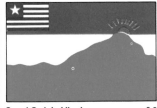

Grand Gedeh, Liberia   2:3

Lower Saxony, West Germany   2:3

North Kordofan, Sudan   2:3

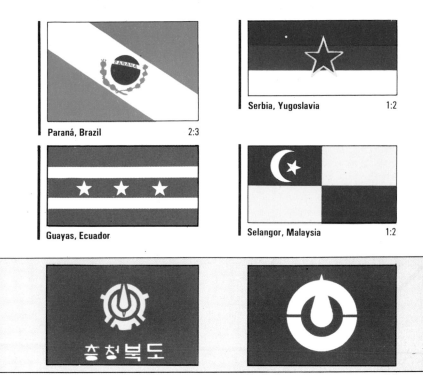

Paraná, Brazil 2:3

Serbia, Yugoslavia 1:2

Guayas, Ecuador

Selangor, Malaysia 1:2

North Chungchong, South Korea 2:3

Kochi, Japan 2:3

from them either at the time or later. Apart from the very varied Swiss cantonal flags, which date from as early as the 13th century, regional flags with heraldic designs have been adopted by provinces of such countries as Belgium, Holland, Norway and Canada. Characteristic of many of the Belgian flags is the lion rampant, seen in the flag of Brabant opposite. Other heraldic symbols are displayed in the wide range of designs created for Norwegian county flags.

Heraldic shields rather than objects decorate the often striped regional flags of West Germany, such as the flag of Lower Saxony illustrated on the left, while state seals form the central emblem in flags flown by the provinces of the Philippines and some of the states of the United States.

In the East, beautiful modern emblems that echo western heraldic devices are seen on the flags adopted by South Korean provinces and Japanese prefectures after World War II. Representational objects are prominent in flags flown by Liberian counties and Sudanese provinces.

As well as emblems and symbols, provincial flags may also use colours that have some historical significance for the region. The blue and white of Ecuador's Guayas province, for example, recall the colours of revolutionary flags seen in Central and South America in the early 19th century. Striped designs have been created for many sub-national flags around the world. They can be seen, for example, in Brazil, Colombia, Malaysia, the Soviet Union and Yugoslavia.

33

CITY FLAGS

In most countries of the world the national or state flag is the only flag to be seen flying over public buildings. In Europe, however, many old cities have had their own flags for many centuries, and some of these have even had a role to play in their country's history. The blue and red flag of Paris, for instance, became the basis of the present French flag in the Revolution of 1789. The flag of New York, too, reveals its historical origins in the orange, white and blue tricolour of the first Dutch settlers. Below are just a few of the many beautiful city flags still flying around the world today.

The official flag of Amsterdam has stripes in colours derived from the shield in the central coat-of-arms.

Flags of some cities

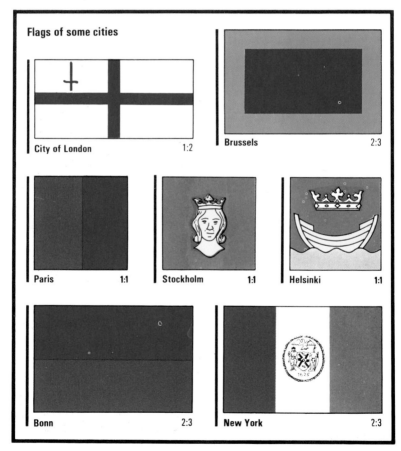

City of London   1:2

Brussels   2:3

Paris   1:1

Stockholm   1:1

Helsinki   1:1

Bonn   2:3

New York   2:3

Yacht Club of Italy

The house flag of British Rail seen on the funnel of its ships.

Pennant of the French Legion of Honour

International Federation of Vexillological Associations   2:3

Workers' organizations and trades unions around the world often display elaborate banners expressing their ideals in symbolical form

FLAGS OF ORGANIZATIONS

Just as nations have created flags to indicate their unity, so have smaller groups of people chosen symbols to express their identity. Social and sporting clubs, professional associations, commercial companies and many other kinds of organizations throughout the world have adopted flags for display over their buildings. Member of trade unions, too, carry elaborate banners proclaiming their brotherhood. At sea can be seen the triangular *burgees* that identify yacht clubs and, boldly displayed on ships' funnels, the emblems of shipping lines and commercial companies.

Flag of MENSA   2:3

World Scout flag   2:3

Olympic Flag   2:3

United Nations   2:3

INTERNATIONAL FLAGS

Some of the flags seen around the world today are those of international organizations with world-wide interests. Perhaps the best known is the pale blue flag of the United Nations Organization. In the centre is its white emblem, consisting of a globe symbolizing the organization's international status and two olive branches representing its aim to ensure world-wide peace. The flag was adopted in 1947 following the formation of the

organization after World War II.

Another well-known flag has been flown at the Olympic Games since 1920, when it was hoisted at the Antwerp Games. The five interlinked rings, in blue, yellow, black, green and red, stand for the five continents and for friendship between them, and have been used as the symbol of the Olympic Games since 1906.

While the flags of the United Nations and the Olympic Games are essentially symbols of organizations striving for peace and understanding, the flags used by the Red Cross, Red Crescent, Red Magen David and Soviet Red

Organization of   2:3
African Unity

Organization of   2:3
American States

League of Arab States   1:2

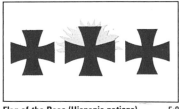

Flag of the Race (Hispanic nations)   5:9

The flag of the Olympic Games flies over the stadium in Munich during the Games of 1972

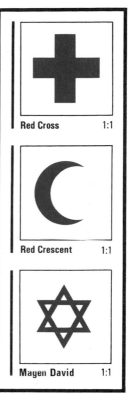

Red Cross   1:1

Red Crescent   1:1

Magen David   1:1

Cross were created as a result of the suffering brought about by war. An international conference held in Geneva in 1863 laid down guidelines to ensure that, in wartime, hospitals and people engaged in caring for the wounded would be regarded as neutral by both sides. The symbol chosen to mark hospitals and medical vehicles in areas where Christian armies were at war was the Swiss flag with its colours reversed to make a red cross on a white field. The organization thus came to be known as the Red Cross.

In Muslim countries the appropriate parallel symbol to the Christian red cross was the red crescent, while in Iran the traditional emblem of the country, the lion and sun, was chosen since its people were followers of a different sect of Islam. In the Soviet Union the flag displays a red cross and crescent side by side.

Other international flags denote particular regional groupings of countries with political, economic or cultural links. The Council of Europe, for example, flies a sky blue flag with a circle of 12 gold stars in the centre as its emblem.

The flags of other regional groups are illustrated on the left. The Organization of African Unity uses a flag with a central emblem containing a map of the continent. Other appropriate emblems are seen in the flags flown by the League of Arab States and the Organization of American States. An interesting design appears in the Flag of the Race flown by Spanish-speaking countries to symbolize their cultural ties.

FLAGS THROUGH HISTORY

The following pages provide a guide to general trends and stages in the development of flags throughout the world and describe some of the more famous flags of the past. More details on the historical background of individual national flags can be found on pages 53–123.

190

STANDARD

OF SARDINIA

Merchant *the same as* Kingdom *without the Crown*.

191

Kingdom of Sardinia

192

Island of Sardinia

193

Sardinian Signal for a Pilot

194

Monaco

195

Lucca.

196

Carrara

197

Genoa

198

Nice

THE WORLD'S FIRST FLAGS

No-one knows when, or by whom, the first flag in history was raised. It is doubtful if any one person was in fact responsible, for flags seem to have been developed by various peoples all over the world at a time when contact between them was unlikely.

Just as they discovered fire, our distant ancestors may have realized that by fastening a piece of animal fur to a stick they could make an effective means of signalling. Centuries later, at the sea battle of Salamis in 480 BC, the Greek commander Themistocles is said to have hoisted a red cloak on an oar and so rallied his forces that they won a great victory over the Persian fleet.

But even before then the great civilizations of Asia had devised various kinds of standards, called *vexilloids*, in wood, metal, leather and other materials and generally consisting of a staff with emblems attached to it. The emblems were devised to represent the gods, whose spiritual power entered the standards and, when carried into battle, guaranteed protection and victory.

Flags as we know them today – pieces of cloth attached laterally to a staff – were created by the Chinese as early as 3000 BC. These Chinese flags were made of silk and, as elsewhere, were used for military and religious purposes.

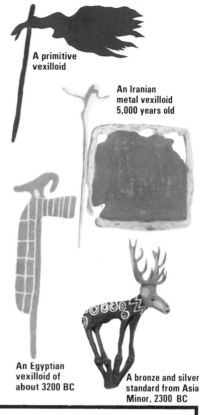

A primitive vexilloid

An Iranian metal vexilloid 5,000 years old

An Egyptian vexilloid of about 3200 BC

A bronze and silver standard from Asia Minor, 2300 BC

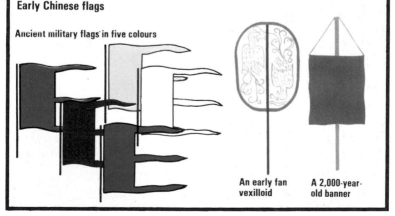

Early Chinese flags

Ancient military flags in five colours

An early fan vexilloid

A 2,000-year-old banner

Flags of the early 19th century are illustrated on a page from a flag book published in 1853.

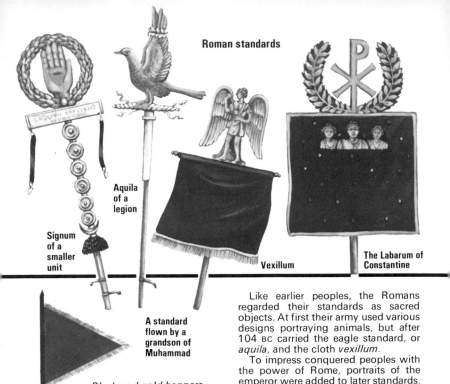

Roman standards

Signum of a smaller unit

Aquila of a legion

Vexillum

The Labarum of Constantine

A standard flown by a grandson of Muhammad

Black and gold banners are illustrated in a 13th-century Islamic manuscript

Like earlier peoples, the Romans regarded their standards as sacred objects. At first their army used various designs portraying animals, but after 104 BC carried the eagle standard, or *aquila*, and the cloth *vexillum*.

To impress conquered peoples with the power of Rome, portraits of the emperor were added to later standards. In this way, the religious and political symbolism of the standards was reinforced. The Labarum which the emperor Constantine created in AD 312 to commemorate his conversion to Christianity not only displayed his portrait but also, on the staff, the X and P symbols of Christ. Religious and earthly authority were thus united in this powerful political flag.

In the 6th century a new religious force in the form of Islam appeared in Arabia. The green turban and black and white banners which its founder, Muhammad, is said to have used, influenced the colours of the flags adopted by his successors. As Islam spread over the Middle East and North Africa, specific colours came to be associated with the most powerful ruling families. Red, white, black and, of course, green predominated. Banners of complex designs also appeared, often incorporating Arabic inscriptions into ornate abstract patterns of great beauty.

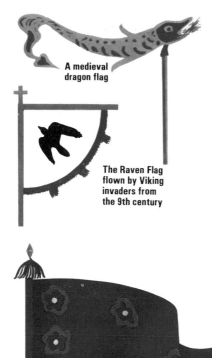

A medieval dragon flag

The Raven Flag flown by Viking invaders from the 9th century

The Oriflamme of Charlemagne

The standard of Genghis Khan displays his personal emblem, a gyrfalcon

EARLY MEDIEVAL FLAGS

Throughout the Middle Ages, vexilloids of all kinds appeared in various parts of the world. One particular creation was widely used with terrifying effect on the field of battle. This was the aptly named dragon flag, shaped like a windsock and often containing a device that whistled when the wind blew through it. A dragon flag was carried by the English forces of King Harold at the battle of Hastings in 1066.

Pennants attached to the lances of knights came into use as identifying emblems in European wars during this period. At the same time, images of saints were carried into battle to aid and protect the soldiers who fought under them. For 850 years after the battle of Vouillé in AD 507, French troops carried replicas of the blue cloak which St Martin is said to have shared with a beggar. The same intense religious feeling surrounded the flags used by both sides during the long Christian reconquest of Spain from the Muslim Moors which ended in 1492.

During this period another historic flag appeared in central Europe, the bright orange-red colour of which earned it the name of the Oriflamme of Charlemagne. Its shape was that of the gonfanon, which was widely used at that time.

In the centuries following Charlemagne's reign, two flags in particular became symbols of terror for the peoples who came face to face with them. One was the Raven Flag carried by Viking invaders in Europe after AD 878. The other was the standard of the Mongol leader Genghis Khan, whose armies swept across Asia in the early 13th century.

41

MEDIEVAL GUILD BANNERS

Until the Middle Ages, the use of flags was the prerogative of kings and nobles. The only banners which ordinary people could perhaps claim as their own were the images of saints which they carried on feast days or in times of war. From the 11th century, however, merchants and craftsmen in some European towns banded together to form guilds that controlled local trade. Each guild, such as the goldsmiths, the drapers or the vintners, had its own distinctive emblem which it displayed on its banner.

The banner of a medieval guild of blacksmiths displays a suitable emblem.

A blood-stained tunic in a medieval battle, left, gave rise to the red and white stripes in the Austrian flag, below.

THE EMERGENCE OF HERALDRY

In the thick of the fighting during the battle of Hastings in 1066, William the Conqueror suddenly raised the visor of his helmet to let his soldiers see that he was still alive. His gesture was symptomatic of the pressing need for some form of easy identification on the battlefield. The flags carried by both sides in this battle were almost meaningless as identifying emblems. The dragon flag of the English army was used throughout the known medieval world, while the Christian cross flown by the Normans could be claimed equally by both sides.

It was a problem that also occurred in the growing sport of jousting, in which elaborate helmets completely hid the faces of the participants. The solution devised by the court heralds was to have identifying emblems, or *cognizances*, painted on the competitors' shields. A wide range of such emblems appeared on the shields, surcoats and

The flag of the Knights of St John

The eagle emblem of the sultan Saladin

The banner of King Richard I

French troops display their national emblems in a medieval battle

Flags of Japanese samurai

flags of the kings and nobles who, from 1096, took part in various Christian Crusades to free the Holy Places in Palestine from Islamic control. The same designs were also frequently displayed on the clothing of their troops. By about 1150 the code of rules known as *heraldry* had come into existence as a means of regulating the use of all these symbols.

As well as the vast array of devices that identified individual contingents in the Crusades, the Christian cross was a universal symbol that linked all the Christian forces. It was also the emblem of the Knights of St John and the Teutonic Knights, two of the great Christian orders of knights in Jerusalem. Eventually such confusion arose in the colours used in these flags by the various units that in 1188 specific colour schemes were laid down for the flags flown by English, French and Flemish troops.

During these years the shapes of flags also changed. The old many-tailed gonfanon fell out of use as more practical shapes appeared. The most common were the short, pointed *pennon*, the long, tapering *pennant* and the rectangular or square *banner*. Among the latter were the flag of Richard the Lion Heart and the original banner of France.

In Japan, a system similar to western heraldry came into existence in the Middle Ages to regulate the *mon* emblems adopted by important families and the wide range of flag designs used by samurai warriors.

The original banner of France

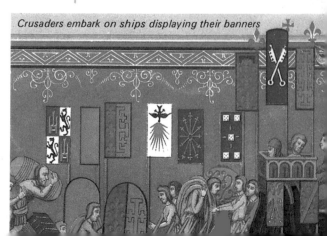

Crusaders embark on ships displaying their banners

Merchant ships from ports belonging to the Hanseatic League flew flags with characteristic emblems, such as the white crosses of Danzig, above.

Navigational maps called portolanos appeared from the 14th century for use on ships. Some of the flags portrayed on them, however, were purely imaginary

The flag of the port of Genoa displayed the cross of St George, its patron saint, in medieval times.

EARLY FLAGS AT SEA

In the Middle Ages, ships carrying soldiers across the seas around Europe indicated their nationality by the various emblems they displayed. Huge symbolic devices appeared on the sails, and painted shields belonging to the knights on board were fixed to the gunwales. At the masthead flew the banner of the king or the nobleman in command.

Merchant ships generally hoisted a streamer in the colours of their home port and sometimes the pennant of their owner. In the Baltic and North seas were seen the red heraldic flags of ports of the Hanseatic League, while the flag of Genoa was one of the best-known emblems in the Mediterranean.

14TH- AND 15TH-CENTURY FLAGS

After the end of the Crusades the heraldic devices on the shields of European nobles were passed on from father to son. Further embellishments in the form of crests, supporters and mottoes were added by heralds to create impressive *coats-of-arms* that effectively showed the superior social status of their owners over other mortals. It is thus not surprising that flags of this period show the great influence of heraldry.

The banner of Spain on page 17 reflects a political event: the union of

The banner of King Edward III.

The standard of Joan of Arc

the kingdoms of Castile and León, indicated by combining their heraldic emblems in the one flag. The banner of Edward III of England, on the other hand, reflected, not a reality, but rather a wish – to see England and France united under one monarch, himself. It was a claim to the French throne that kept the *fleur-de-lis* in the British royal standard until 1801.

A major opponent of England's rule in France in the early 15th century was Joan of Arc, whose white standard gave her country a new national and royal colour that continued beyond the Revolution of 1789.

Even more enduring has been one of Europe's best-known heraldic emblems: the double-headed eagle which appeared on the golden yellow banner of the Holy Roman Empire from the 13th century. Its history goes back, however, to the time of Charlemagne, and its influence continues in the arms and flags of West Germany and Austria. A non-survivor was the 14th-century banner of the old Byzantine Empire.

The double-headed eagle emblem of the Holy Roman Empire

The flag of the Byzantine Empire

FLAGS OF THE 16TH CENTURY

The 16th century saw the beginning of a new era of world exploration. The epic adventure started in 1492, when Christopher Columbus first set foot on the island of El Salvador in the Bahamas, flew the personal standard of King Ferdinand and Queen Isabella of Spain and initiated the conquest of a whole new continent. Within 50 years, the simple red banner of Cortés and the ornate heraldic flag of Pizarro presided over the destruction of the entire Aztec and Inca empires.

In Europe itself, the 16th century witnessed not only the struggle against the Muslim Turks but also the great ideological clash between the Protestant Reformation and the Catholic Counter-reformation. In addition to heraldic banners, Europe now had elaborate standards displaying complex allegorical scenes in which particular causes were seen emerging

Flags carried to the New World by Hernando Cortés, top, and Christopher Columbus, below

triumphant. Such a flag was the standard of the Holy Roman Emperor Charles V.

During this century certain emblems and colours became associated with particular dynasties. White, for example, was the colour of both the powerful Hapsburg and Bourbon families. Upon it, the Spanish Hapsburgs displayed the red saltire of Burgundy.

A German peasant revolt standard of the 1520s, top left, contrasts with the ornate flags used by King Francis I of France, centre, and the Emperor Charles V, below left, during the same years.

Two of the Russian flags created by Peter the Great about 1700.

Flags decorate the European ships that defeated the Turks at the battle of Lepanto in 1571

FLAGS AT SEA SINCE 1500

During the 16th century, ships ventured farther and farther afield on great voyages of discovery, and flags indicating their ownership and nationality became important. At first, huge and impressive flags bearing the royal coat-of-arms were flown from the masthead or stern for prestige and protection. The imposing effect was reinforced by the use of long streamers in the king's livery colours and, on special occasions, by lines of heraldic shields, called *pavis-ades*, along the ship's sides. Displays of this sort were seen, for instance, when Henry VIII of England sailed to meet Francis I of France, or when the Spanish Armada sailed on its ill-fated venture against England in 1588.

As time passed, the difficulty of identifying the nationality of ships flying such ornate flags led to an increasing use of simpler designs. English ships, for example, came to be recognized from the 16th century by the St George's cross on a white flag, while French vessels flew various designs, including blue flags with either a white cross or three gold *fleurs-de-lis*. Dutch ships displayed striped flags in orange (later red), white and blue.

From the mid-17th century, flags with a quarterly red and white design divided by a blue cross were seen on Russian ships. Then, in the 1690s, Peter the Great, the Tsar of Russia, set out to make his country a great naval power and personally designed a selection of flags in red, white and blue for his ships. His final choice, a blue saltire on a white field, was used until 1917.

During this period, the nationality of ships came to be indicated by a *jack* at the prow and an *ensign* at the stern (see also pages 28–29).

Flags bearing the traditional Sun Disc emblem appear on a 17th-century Japanese warship.

47

THE BIRTH OF NATIONAL FLAGS

Many of the national flags seen around the world today have evolved over a long period of time. The flags of countries such as Austria, Denmark or Turkey emerged from the mists of legend while many others, including those of Poland and Switzerland, grew out of the heraldic emblems of the Middle Ages. The 17th century saw the

The revolutionary Dutch flag

birth of several national flags through revolutionary struggle. One of these was the flag of the Netherlands, which appeared during the 80-year Dutch rebellion which began in 1568 against Spanish domination. The Dutch war cry 'Orange on top' was a reference not only to their leader, William I, Prince of Orange, but also to the colours of their flag, a horizontal tricolour of orange, white and blue stripes. This flag, with the orange stripe subsequently changed to red, has been the national flag of the Netherlands ever since.

The 'Union Jack' of the United Kingdom had a more peaceful evolution. The process began in 1603, when England and Scotland were

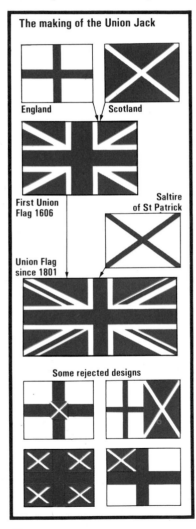

The making of the Union Jack

England

Scotland

First Union Flag 1606

Saltire of St Patrick

Union Flag since 1801

Some rejected designs

The banner of Oliver Cromwell

united under one ruler, King James I (VI of Scotland). Three years later, James decreed that the flag of the new united kingdom should be the red St George's cross of England combined with the white St Andrew's cross of Scotland. All kinds of designs to meet this requirement were proposed, and rejected, before the first Union Flag was finally chosen. It was not until 1801, however, that the so-called cross of St Patrick was incorporated into the design to make the present well-known 'Union Jack'.

The state flag of France, 1640s-1790

Bastille flag, 1789

The revolutionary cockade of 1789

French national colours, 1790.

The emergence of the French tricolour

The American 'Stars and Stripes' emerged in the violence of the revolutionary war of 1775–83, in which Britain's 13 colonies in New England broke away from the mother country. A tradition of rebel flags, however, had already been established in America. Over a century earlier, Puritan settlers had objected to the 'papish' St George's cross in the British Red Ensign flown in the colonies, and a red flag with a plain white canton was flown instead. A few decades later, further dissension led to the addition of a pine tree emblem to this flag, a design with local significance.

In the 1760s, as agitation mounted against British rule, flags displaying all kinds of rebel slogans appeared. Within months of the outbreak of the revolution in 1775, the Americans adopted an unofficial flag of their own, known as the Continental Colours, which they used until 1777. In that year they replaced it with the first 'Stars and Stripes', which had in the canton, instead of the British Union Flag, 13 stars to represent the 13 former colonies. Since then the number of states, and stars in the flag, has grown to 50.

Another revolution created the national flag of France. The dramatic storming of the prison-fortress of the Bastille on 14 July 1789 began the events that ousted the monarchy and changed the French flag. The colours adopted by the revolutionary regime were the traditional white of France with the blue and red of Paris. They were seen in several flags before the present tricolour emerged in 1794.

American revolutionary flags

The Bedford Flag, flown on the first day of the revolution, 1775

The pine tree flag

The Continental Colours

The first Stars and Stripes

49

FLAGS OF THE 19TH CENTURY

Political · change and social reform, allied to a growing sense of nationhood among ordinary people, led to the birth of new nations and flags all over the world in the 19th and 20th centuries. Revolution against Spanish and Portuguese colonial rule, for example, created the flags now flown by independent nations in South and Central America. One of the first symbols in this struggle was the banner portraying the Virgin of Guadalupe hoisted in Mexico in 1810.

A fight for national unification in the 19th century eventually produced the basic design of the flags flown today in Italy and the two German states.

Alternative Russian civil flags before 1914

A German unification flag, 1832

The flag of unified Italy, 1861-1946

Mexico's Virgin of Guadalupe banner

Germany's rebirth was the purpose expressed by the flag unfurled in 1832 by students agitating for German unification. Another tricolour, created in the 1790s and adopted in 1848 by the kingdom of Sardinia, became the national flag of a new, united Italy in 1861.

Elsewhere in the world at this time, different forms of struggle created other flags, some short-lived, others surviving today. One of the latter is the flag flown by the Confederate southern states in the American Civil War of 1861-5. On the other side of the world, pressure upon China to adopt western conventions led to the appearance of flags imposed by Europeans. Among these were the blue and yellow dragon flags that represented China from 1872 to 1912.

The battle flag of the southern states in the American Civil War

The state flag of China, 1872-90

50

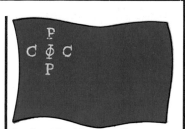

Russian national flag, 1918-20

After the Russian revolution of 1917 red flags with gold inscriptions replaced the flags of the tsarist regime.

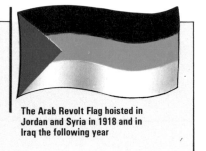

The Arab Revolt Flag hoisted in Jordan and Syria in 1918 and in Iraq the following year

While some nations gained freedom, others were forced, even though temporarily, to surrender it to the fascist regimes that emerged in Italy, Germany and Japan during the 20s and 30s. German flags of this time displayed the ancient *swastika* symbol, which, according to the nation's leader Adolf Hitler, represented the revival of German greatness. World War II, however, ended with the defeat of Germany and the disappearance of its flags.

Since the war, the dismemberment of the old colonial empires of Britain, France and Portugal has created many new, independent nations, particularly in Africa, where a rich collection of flags is still evolving.

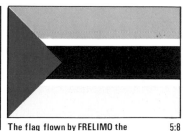

The flag flown by FRELIMO the Mozambique liberation movement prior to independence in 1975   5:8

Somali women take part in a national parade.

FLAGS OF OUR TIME

With the appearance of fresh ideologies and newly independent nations, many new flags have emerged in the 20th century. One of the first to appear, and one of the most influential ever since, was the Red Flag of the Soviet Union, which replaced all the old emblems of tsarist Russia after the revolution of 1917. At about the same time, another red flag – that of the Ottoman Empire, which had flown over much of the Middle East and North Africa since the 16th century – was under fierce attack as the Arab nations under its domination began the struggle for their freedom. From 1918 the Arab Revolt Flag, in the traditional colours of Islam, appeared in Jordan, Syria and Iraq. Since then it has been a major influence on many other Arab flags in that part of the world.

FLAGS OF EUROPE

Most of the national flags illustrated on the following pages are the civil flags used by private citizens. Where these do not exist, the state, or government flags have been included. The proportions of each flag are indicated as a ratio of the width, or breadth, to the length.

FINLAND

Finland became an independent republic only in 1917 after separation from Russia, which was then in the throes of the Bolshevik revolution. The present civil flag was adopted soon after and, according to tradition, was based on a design proposed by the poet Sakari Topelius in about 1860. It has a light blue Scandinavian cross (a cross offset towards the hoist) on a white field, the colours symbolizing Finland's blue lakes and white snow.

At the centre of the cross the state flag bears the national coat-of-arms, consisting of a yellow lion rampant holding a sword and standing on an oriental scimitar, all upon a red field.

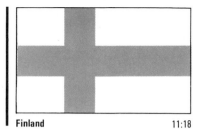

Finland   11:18

ALAND ISLANDS

This autonomous group of Finnish islands in the Baltic Sea has had its own official flag since 1954. Its design is a red Scandinavian cross fimbriated in yellow and standing on a light blue field. The flag may be flown only on the islands, not at sea. On official buildings it may only be flown if hoisted below a Finnish flag larger in size.

Aland Islands   17:26

SWEDEN

The Swedish national flag has been flown since the reign of King Gustavus Vasa in the early 16th century. The design, however, was not officially established until 1906. It is a golden yellow Scandinavian cross on a blue field. The colours were derived from the ancient state coat-of-arms dating from 1364, which bears three golden yellow crowns on a blue field. The cross also probably originated in the same arms.

Sweden   5:8

NORWAY

After being ruled by Denmark from the 14th century until 1814 and then united with Sweden for nearly a century, Norway became an independent country only in 1905. The present national flag shows the country's long link with Denmark and reflects the design and colours of the Danish *Dannebrog* flag, to which has been added a blue cross over the white of the Danish flag. This design appeared in 1821 as the Norwegian merchant flag, but restrictions on its use at sea were not lifted until 1898.

Norway   8:11

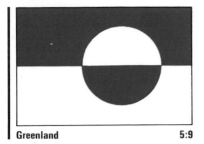

Greenland 5:9

Denmark 28:37

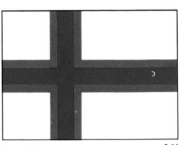

Faroe Islands 8:11

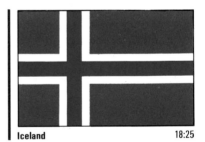

Iceland 18:25

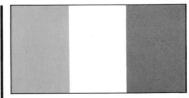

Ireland 1:2

GREENLAND
A local flag for use in Greenland was adopted in June 1985. It portrays the rising sun, but continues to use the colours of Denmark.

DENMARK
A white cross on a red field is the design of the Danish national flag, known as the *Dannebrog* (the spirit of Denmark). It may be the oldest national flag to have been used continuously. The flag may originally have been one of the many similar flags flown by the nobles of the Holy Roman Empire in the border territories during the Middle Ages, or have been a gift from a medieval pope to a Christian king fighting against pagans in the north.

ICELAND
The design of the Icelandic flag identifies it as one of the Scandinavian group. It became the official national flag when Iceland gained independence from Denmark in 1944.

FAROE ISLANDS
Officially adopted in 1948, the national and merchant flag of the Faroe Islands, which are part of Denmark, is a red cross fimbriated in blue on a white field. As in other Scandinavian flags, the upright limb of the cross is placed towards the hoist.

IRELAND
The present Irish flag was inspired by the tricolour of the French Revolution and was first used by Irish nationalists in 1848 as an unofficial symbol in the struggle for freedom from Britain. It became the official national flag of Ireland in 1922, after independence.

54

UNITED KINGDOM

Although it is commonly accepted that the 'Union Jack' is the state flag, the United Kingdom, in fact, has no official national flag for use by private citizens. The 'Union Jack' is really a royal flag which the British Parliament has stated can be flown by private persons, but only on land. The term 'Union Jack' is strictly incorrect, since a jack is for use only at the prow of a ship; the correct name is 'Union Flag'.

The Union Flag is a combination of flags representing the main parts of the United Kingdom, excepting Wales. The process began in 1603 when James VI of Scotland became also James I of England and ordered an appropriate flag to be designed. The result was the red St George's cross of England, fimbriated in white, with the St Andrew's saltire of Scotland as its field.

The so-called cross of St Patrick was incorporated into the Union Flag in 1801, when Ireland was united with Great Britain. The red saltire on a white field was, in fact, the heraldic device of the Fitzgerald family, who were sent to subjugate Ireland by Henry II of England, and it has never been used by

United Kingdom　　　　　　　　　　1:2

the Irish as their emblem. The saltire is counterchanged to give Scotland precedence in the flag.

WALES

The flag of Wales did not form part of the Union Flag, since the country was annexed much earlier by Edward I and thus became part of the kingdom of England. However, the Welsh do have their own traditional flag and it was officially recognized in 1959. It is the red dragon of Cadwallader, Prince of Gwynedd, on a field divided horizontally white over green and representing the livery colours of the Welsh Prince Llewelyn and, later, of all the Tudor monarchs.

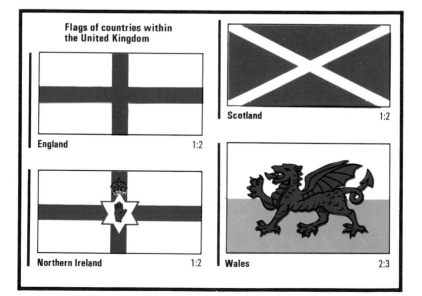

Flags of countries within the United Kingdom

England　　　　　　　　　　1:2

Northern Ireland　　　　　　　　1:2

Scotland　　　　　　　　　　1:2

Wales　　　　　　　　　　2:3

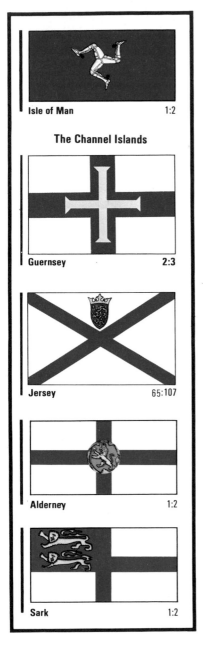

Isle of Man 1:2

The Channel Islands

Guernsey 2:3

Jersey 65:107

Alderney 1:2

Sark 1:2

NORTHERN IRELAND
Although the Union Flag is the official national emblem of Northern Ireland, the region has its own semi-official flag, a St George's cross on a white field (see page 55). In the centre is a six-pointed white star, representing the six counties of Northern Ireland, charged with a red hand, the traditional emblem of the province of Ulster. Above the star is a royal crown.

THE ISLE OF MAN
This semi-independent island in the Irish Sea has its own national flag which is flown on official buildings and by private citizens on land. Its design is the traditional *trinacria* symbol, dating from the 13th century, on a red field. The trinacria consists of three legs joined at the thigh and running in a clockwise direction on both the obverse and reverse sides of the flag. The Manx merchant flag is the British Red Ensign defaced by the trinacria.

THE CHANNEL ISLANDS
This group of islands in the English Channel includes four main islands, each of which has its own flag.

Guernsey. A new flag was adopted in 1985 which added the cross from the flag of William the Conqueror to the traditional cross of St George.

Jersey has a flag like the saltire flag of St Patrick, but in 1981 a small crowned shield with the arms of Jersey was added.

Alderney, a dependency of Guernsey, flies, on official buildings only, a red St George's cross on a white field. In the centre of the cross is a circular badge containing a crowned lion rampant holding a leafy twig upon a green field surrounded with a gold border. After long unofficial use, the flag was finally approved in 1906.

Sark has no official flag, but the ruling Seigneur or Dame of the island flies a curious flag which is part personal banner and part state flag. It is a St George's cross with the canton in red, upon which are two gold lions from the arms of the Duchy of Normandy.

France   2:3

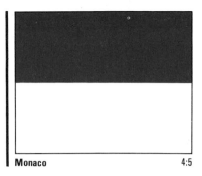

Monaco   4:5

FRANCE

The present national flag of France, the blue, white and red tricolour, is one of the best-known flags in the world. Its design of vertical stripes originated in the French Revolution of 1789 and may have been based on the revolutionary Dutch flag or on the red and blue colours of Paris combined with the white of the Bourbon family. Starting at the hoist, the order of colours was at first red, white and blue, but the present arrangement was adopted in 1794.

The width of the stripes has varied over the years. To give the visual effect of equal width at sea, the red stripe is wider than the white, which in turn is wider than the blue.

MONACO

An independent state since AD 980, Monaco has been ruled by the Grimaldi family since 1297. The red and white lozenges in the shield of the Prince of Monaco's coat-of-arms provided the colours for the national flag. The design of the flag, officially adopted in 1881, is halved horizontally red over white like the more recent flag of Indonesia.

LUXEMBOURG

The Grand Duchy of Luxembourg has a national flag which is almost identical to that of the Netherlands, except that the blue stripe is of a lighter shade and the flag is longer. The red, white and blue colours were derived from the Grand Duke's · coat-of-arms, which dates from the 13th century.

BELGIUM

A vertical tricolour of black, gold and red, almost square in shape, is the national flag of Belgium. These were the colours of a horizontally striped flag which appeared when the province of Brabant rose up against Austrian rule in 1787. The present vertical design was adopted as the national flag in 1830 when Belgium gained its independence from the Netherlands.

Luxembourg   3:5

Belgium   13:15

THE NETHERLANDS

The national flag of the Netherlands, with its horizontal stripes of red, white and blue, dates from 1630, during the 80-year war of independence from Spain that began in 1568. Prior to 1630 the Dutch rebels flew the orange, white and blue colours of their leader, William I, Prince of Orange. Today Dutch citizens are permitted to fly an orange pennant above the tricolour on occasions of national importance.

The Dutch tricolour became a symbol of liberty and inspired other revolutionary flags around the world, perhaps including that of France. The proportions and colours of the present flag were officially established in 1937.

WEST GERMANY

The Federal Republic of Germany (West Germany) flies a national flag with horizontal stripes of black, red and gold, colours associated with the struggle for a united Germany from the 1830s. On its state flag, West Germany uses a black eagle in a gold shield placed slightly towards the hoist. The flag was officially adopted in 1949.

AUSTRIA

A tricolour with equal, horizontal stripes of red, white and red is the national flag of Austria. The state flag has the state arms, a black eagle wearing broken chains, in the centre. This flag first appeared in 1786. The design without the central emblem used as the national flag today was adopted by the first republic after 1918 and re-adopted by the second republic in 1945, after World War II.

According to tradition, the red and white colours of the Austrian flag originated in the blood-stained tunic of Leopold, Duke of Babenberg, who fought in the battle of Ptolemais in 1191. The only part of his tunic unstained by blood was the white stripe around his waist where his sword-belt had been.

LIECHTENSTEIN

The national flag of the principality of Liechtenstein has two equal, horizontal stripes, royal blue over red. In the blue stripe, at the hoist, is a gold crown, which is often seen turned 90° so that the flag can be hung vertically.

Netherlands   2:3

Austria   2:3

West Germany   3:5

Liechtenstein   2:3

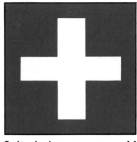

Switzerland 1:1

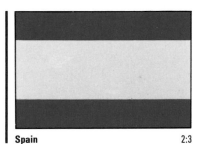

Spain 2:3

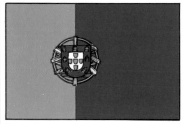

Portugal 2:3

Andorra 2:3

SWITZERLAND
A square flag bearing a white Greek cross on a red field has been the official national flag of the Swiss confederation since 1848. But the use of this emblem by the Swiss goes back many centuries. A medieval chronicle describes Swiss soldiers marching out to fight oppressive rulers in 1339 wearing a distinguishing emblem, 'the sign of the Holy Cross, a white cross on a red shield'. The same emblem appears in the rectangular merchant flag used on the nation's lakes and the River Rhine.

PORTUGAL
Portugal's leading role in discovering the world beyond Europe's boundaries in the 15th and 16th centuries has been recognized in the country's national flag since 1815. Behind the state coat-of-arms is an armillary sphere, an early navigational instrument. The field behind the emblem is divided vertically into two stripes, a green one representing Prince Henry the Navigator (1394–1460) next to the hoist, and a

red one half as wide again representing the monarchy in the fly. The design dates from 1910, when Portugal became a republic.

SPAIN
When Charles III of Spain adopted a striped red and yellow flag for his ships in 1785, he was simply reinstating the traditional colours of Spain unused since the time of the 15th-century Catholic monarchs, Ferdinand and Isabella. The colours were, in fact, those of the old kingdom of Aragon as early as the 12th century.

The present national flag, in which the central yellow stripe is twice as wide as each of the red stripes, was introduced in 1938. The national coat-of-arms often appears in the hoist.

ANDORRA
In the tiny Pyrenean state of Andorra, blue, gold and red-striped flags of various designs can be seen flying. A vertically striped tricolour has been used since 1866, and usually has the state arms in the centre.

Gibraltar 1:2

Malta 2:3

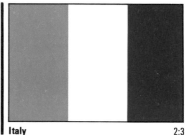

Italy 2:3

Vatican City State 1:1

San Marino 3:4

GIBRALTAR

As a British dependency since 1713, Gibraltar uses the Union Flag of the United Kingdom as its official flag, although the traditional Blue Ensign, with the coat-of-arms of the colony in a white circle in the fly, is also seen. However, an unofficial national flag began to be used by citizens of Gibraltar in 1966, its design based on the Rock's coat-of-arms. This flag has two horizontal stripes, white over red, with the white stripe twice as wide as the red. In the centre is a red, three-towered castle below which is suspended a gold key, a badge which symbolizes Gibraltar's role as a fortress at the entrance to the Mediterranean.

MALTA

The national flag of Malta, adopted when the island group gained independence from Britain in 1964, has two equal vertical stripes of white (near the hoist) and red (in the fly). In the upper hoist, fimbriated in red, is a representation of the George Cross medal awarded by Britain to the people of the islands for their heroism during World War II. Permission to add the medal to the flag and arms of Malta was granted by Britain in 1943.

The colours of the Maltese flag are traditionally said to date back to the banner of a cousin of William the Conquerer, Count William the Norman, who liberated the islands from Muslim rule in 1090. The same colours were used for the flag of the Knights Hospitallers, later known as the Knights of Malta, who ruled the islands from 1530 to 1798. Their flag was a white cross on a red field. Their badge, a four-armed, eight-pointed star, can still be seen in the present white and red Maltese merchant flag.

ITALY

The present design of the tricolour used as the national flag of Italy dates from 1946. But the history of the Italian tricolour goes back to the time of Napoleon's invasion of Italy in 1796. In that year the French established a new Republican National Guard in northern Italy which carried a military standard of vertical green, white and red stripes, a design clearly based on the French tricolour. That same year the Cispadane Republic was set up and it adopted what may be called the first real national flag of Italy, a horizontally striped tricolour in green, white and red and with a coat-of-arms in the centre designed by Napoleon himself.

The tricolour underwent many changes during the tumultuous events of the unification of Italy in the 19th century, but the vertically striped tricolour, identified by the Italian people as a symbol of freedom and unity, finally became established as the national flag in the late 1870s.

VATICAN CITY

Since 1929 the flag of the Vatican City State has been a bicolour of two equal vertical stripes of yellow (or gold) and white. On the white stripe, in the fly, is the emblem used since the 13th century to represent the Vatican's role as the headquarters of the Roman Catholic Church. It consists of the traditional triple tiara of the popes above two crossed keys, one gold and one silver. These represent the keys to the Kingdom of Heaven bestowed by Christ upon St Peter. The gold and white colours of the flag, derived from the keys of St Peter, were officially adopted in 1825.

SAN MARINO

The tiny Republic of San Marino, enclosed completely within the territory of Italy, has been an independent state since AD 885. The snow on the mountain peaks and the blue of the sky above are represented in the colours of the national flag. This has two equal horizontal stripes, white over blue. The state flag has the coat-of-arms of San Marino in the centre.

CYPRUS

Although now divided into two separate communities of Greeks and Turks, Cyprus has an official state flag which was designed to avoid controversy between the two groups. It is a plain white flag with a solid yellow map of the island above two olive branches in the centre. Both the choice of white and the use of the olive branches stress the desire for peace on the island. This flag was officially adopted when Cyprus gained independence from Britain in 1960.

GREECE

Nine horizontal stripes of blue and white, with a white cross on a blue field in the canton, form the design of the Greek national and state flags used since 1822. The nine stripes represent the nine syllables of the Greek phrase meaning 'Freedom or Death', which was used as a battle cry during the struggle against Turkish domination in the 1820s. Blue and white became the national colours during the war of independence.

The old flag of blue with a white cross only is still used unofficially within Greece.

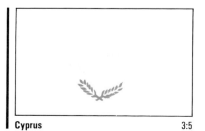

Cyprus   3:5

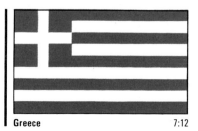

Greece   7:12

Albania 5:7

Yugoslavia 1:2

Bulgaria 3:5

Romania 2:3

ALBANIA
Since 1945 the national flag of Albania has been a dark red flag in the centre of which is a double-headed black eagle surmounted by a red star fimbriated in gold. In the Albanian language the name of the country means 'the land of eagles', and it was an eagle which became the emblem of the 15th-century Albanian patriot Skanderbeg in his struggle against Turkish invaders. His flag was re-adopted by the Albanians when the country finally gained its independence in 1912. Several emblems were used above the eagle on the flag before the red star of Communism was added in 1945.

YUGOSLAVIA
Yugoslavia became an independent state only after World War I, when several previously separate countries united in 1918 to form a new kingdom. The blue, white and red colours in the flags of these former states were incorporated into the national flag of the new country, a tricolour of horizontal stripes bearing a coat-of-arms. In 1946 the coat-of-arms was replaced by a red star, the symbol of Communism. This flag had been used during World War II by patriots led by Josip Broz (later Marshal Tito), and when he came to power his flag was adopted as the official flag of Yugoslavia.

BULGARIA
Bulgaria flies as its national flag a tricolour of white, green and red stripes with the state coat-of-arms in the white stripe near the hoist. The colours were first adopted in 1878 and are said to be symbolic. White stands for a desire for peace and liberty, green for the agricultural wealth of the country and red for the courage of the army. The state emblem on the flag dates, with minor changes, from 1947.

ROMANIA
The national flag of Romania is a tricolour of vertical stripes of blue, gold and red, with the state coat-of-arms representing the country's natural resources in the centre. The tricolour design dates from 1848, when the colours were arranged horizontally. They were changed to vertical in 1866.

HUNGARY

Since 1957 the national flag of Hungary has been a plain tricolour with horizontal stripes of red, white and green. The origins of these colours go back as far as the late 9th century, when a plain red flag was adopted by Árpád, the leader of the Magyar tribe whose dynasty ruled Hungary until 1301. After the Magyars became Christians in the late 10th century, a cross on a white field became the country's flag. By the 15th century, red, white and green had become the colours in the Hungarian arms. By 1848, influenced by the French tricolour, a striped flag in the three colours was already in use and this forms the national flag today.

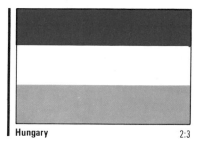

Hungary   2:3

CZECHOSLOVAKIA

The Czech national flag has the red, white and blue colours to be found in other Slavonic flags, but they are arranged in a striking way. While the white and red make two equal, horizontal stripes, the blue forms an equilateral triangle in the hoist.

The red and white came from the 13th-century arms of the kingdom of Bohemia, while blue was one of the colours of Moravia and Slovakia. They came together in a horizontal tricolour used by Slovakia in 1848. The present Czech flag dates from 1920.

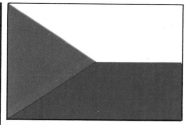

Czechoslovakia   2:3

EAST GERMANY

The arrangement of black, red and gold stripes in the national flag of East Germany is also to be seen in the flag of West Germany. But the East German flag has a state emblem in the centre. As in other Communist countries, this emblem consists of symbols representing the nation's working people – ears of wheat, a hammer and dividers.

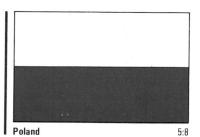

East Germany   3:5

POLAND

The colours of the Polish national flag were derived from the 13th-century state coat-of-arms bearing a white eagle on a red field. These arms appear on the Polish merchant flag and the swallow-tailed naval ensign, but the national and state flag is a plain bicolour of two equal, horizontal stripes, white over red. This flag was created when Poland became an independent republic in 1919.

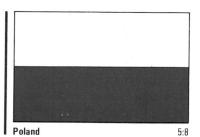

Poland   5:8

Soviet Union   1:2

SOVIET UNION

One of the best-known flags in the world today, the national flag of the Soviet Union, has a simple, but striking design – a plain red flag, in the upper hoist of which is a gold emblem comprising a hammer crossed with a sickle surmounted by a red star fimbriated in gold. The hammer and sickle symbolize the nation's industrial and agricultural workers, while the star represents the rule of the Communist party. This flag is also used as the merchant flag of the Soviet Union. The design has remained basically unchanged since 1923.

The white, blue and red colours of Russian flags used in the time of the tsars until the revolution of 1917 are echoed in the present naval ensign. This is a white flag with a blue stripe along the foot. On the white are a red star and red hammer and sickle. The Soviet army flag is a plain red flag with a central red star fimbriated in gold.

As the official name of the Soviet Union – the Union of Soviet Socialist Republics – implies, the country is made up of a number of separate republics, each of which has its own state flag. These used to be plain red flags with the initials of the republics in the upper hoist. Between 1949 and 1954, however, their designs were changed. In place of the initials, all the new flags adopted the crossed hammer and sickle emblem, but red remained the predominant colour in the fly. These flags are illustrated on the right. One of the most interesting is the flag of the Byelorussian Soviet Socialist Republic, with its pattern of woven cloth in the hoist. The Byelorussian and Ukrainian Soviet Socialist Republics are members of the United Nations Organization in their own right.

Armenian SSR   1:2

Azerbaijan SSR   1:2

Byelorussian SSR   1:2

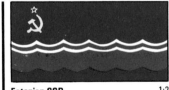

Estonian SSR   1:2

Georgian SSR   1:2

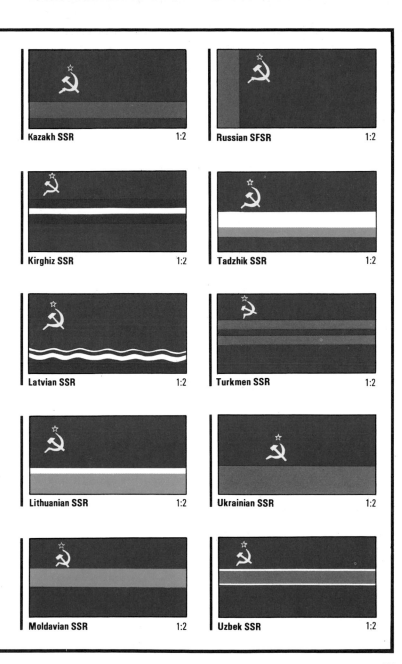

Kazakh SSR 1:2

Russian SFSR 1:2

Kirghiz SSR 1:2

Tadzhik SSR 1:2

Latvian SSR 1:2

Turkmen SSR 1:2

Lithuanian SSR 1:2

Ukrainian SSR 1:2

Moldavian SSR 1:2

Uzbek SSR 1:2

FLAGS OF ASIA

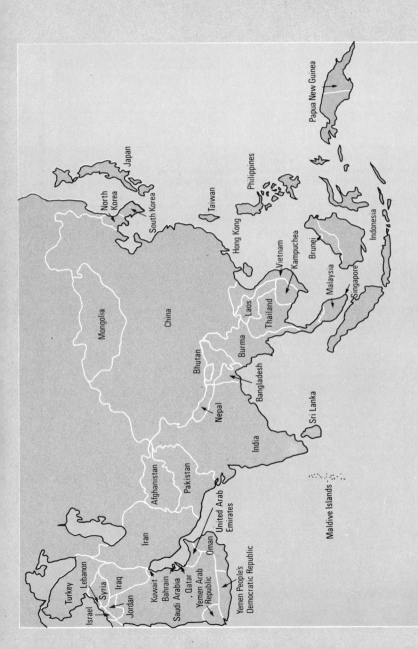

TURKEY

A crescent moon and a five-pointed star, the traditional symbols of Islam, appear in white on the plain red flag of Turkey. Their presence, however, dates from many centuries before Turkey became a Muslim state.

According to one story, the army of King Philip of Macedon tried to capture the city of Byzantium (now Istanbul) in 339 BC by burrowing under the city walls by night. But the crescent moon shone so brightly that the soldiers were discovered and the city was saved. From then on, Byzantium, later renamed Constantinople, used the crescent as its emblem.

Another legend describes a dream of the Muslim Sultan Othman, the first ruler of the Ottoman Turks who invaded what is now Turkey in the late 13th century. He dreamt of a huge crescent moon that shone over the whole world. Thinking this a favourable omen, he adopted the crescent as his symbol.

The star in the flag may be the morning star mentioned in the Koran or the symbol of Christianity added to the crescent flag of Constantinople by the Roman Emperor Constantine.

Turkey   2:3

SYRIA

The flag of Syria is the one adopted in 1958 by the former United Arab Republic. At various times in their history Egypt and Syria have shared the same flag, but since 1980 Syria has used this flag. At one time, the two stars represented Egypt and Syria.

Syria   2:3

LEBANON

Prominent in the centre of the Lebanese national flag is a cedar tree, many of which grow in the country's mountains. Behind the cedar are horizontal stripes of red, white and red, the white being twice the width of each of the red. This flag dates from 1943.

Lebanon   2:3

ISRAEL

As its national flag, Israel flies a design of blue and white stripes based on a Jewish prayer shawl. In the centre is the ancient six-pointed Star of David. The design was made in America in 1891 and was officially adopted by the new state of Israel in 1948.

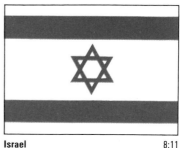

Israel   8:11

JORDAN

The Hashemite Kingdom of Jordan has a national flag that has remained basically the same since 1918, when it was used in the Arab revolt against the Turks. For the present design, adopted in 1921, the sequence of colours in the stripes was changed to black, white and green, and a seven-pointed star was added in the centre of the red triangle in the hoist. The seven points of the star represent the first seven verses of the Koran that form the basis of the Muslim faith.

SAUDI ARABIA

Saudi Arabia has the only national flag with an inscription as its main feature. The inscription, in white on a plain green field, means 'There is no god but Allah, and Muhammad is the Prophet of Allah'. Below it is a white horizontal sword. Green is the traditional colour of the Fatimid dynasty of Arabia established by Muhammad's daughter Fatima. It was chosen because Muhammad reputedly had a green turban. The present design of the flag was adopted in 1938.

The Saudi flag is so constructed that the inscription reads from right to left on both sides whereas the sword points to the hoist on the obverse side and to the fly on the reverse side. This is

Jordan   1:2

Yemen Arab Republic   2:3

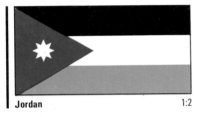

Saudi Arabia   2:3

Yemen People's Democratic Republic   2:3

Oman   2:3

United Arab Emirates   1:2

Qatar 11:28

achieved by sewing two identical flags together. The obverse side is shown in the illustration, although it is conventional in Moslem countries to show the flagstaff on the observer's right.

OMAN
Until 1970, Oman (then called Muscat and Oman) had a plain red flag based on the traditional colour of the Kharijite people who lived in the area. When the new state of Oman was established the state arms, consisting of crossed swords and a dagger, were added to the upper hoist, and stripes of white and green placed in the head and foot of the fly.

YEMEN ARAB REPUBLIC
The horizontally striped red, white and black tricolour of the pan-Arab movement forms the basis of the national flag of the Yemen Arab Republic established in 1962. However, the Yemeni flag has a five-pointed green star in the centre of the white stripe.

PEOPLE'S DEMOCRATIC REPUBLIC OF YEMEN
The red, white and black stripes seen in the national flags of other Arab countries are also to be found in the flag of the People's Democratic Republic of Yemen. However, in the hoist is a pale blue triangle charged with a red star. This flag was adopted in 1967 after the end of British rule from Aden, the country's main port.

UNITED ARAB EMIRATES
When seven small states around the Persian Gulf combined to form the United Arab Emirates in 1971, a flag for the new state had to be designed. The traditional pan-Arab colours of red,

Bahrain 3:5

white, black and green, first seen together in the flag used in the Arab revolt against the Turks from 1916, were chosen. They were arranged as horizontal stripes of green, white and black, with a vertical red stripe in the hoist.

QATAR
Originally Qatar flew a red and white flag, like other Arab states around the Persian Gulf. The present Qatari flag still has a close similarity to that of Bahrain, but since 1949 its colour has been maroon or chocolate, a colour obtained by exposing the natural red dye commonly used in the area to the hot sun. In the hoist is a broad white band, added in about 1866, which is divided from the maroon in the fly by a serrated line. The proportions of the Qatari flag, 11:28, are unique.

BAHRAIN
The traditional red of the Kharijite Muslims living in the lands of eastern Arabia has been preserved in the national flag of Bahrain, together with the white which the British requested to be included in the flags of all friendly Arab states around the Persian Gulf in 1820. The present design dates from about 1932. It has a white stripe in the hoist, divided from the red in the fly by a serrated line.

69

KUWAIT

The national flag of the emirate of Kuwait is another flag bearing the colours associated with pan-Arabism. It has three equal, horizontal stripes of green, white and red, like the flag of neighbouring Iran, but has an unusual black trapezium in the hoist. This may have been inspired by a similar shape in the hoist of Kuwait's other neighbour, Iraq, before 1959. Kuwait's flag dates from 1961, when the country ceased to be a British protectorate.

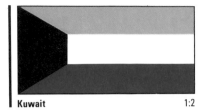

Kuwait   1:2

IRAQ

The four pan-Arab colours – red, white, black and green – appear in the national flag of Iraq. The basic design of horizontal red, white and black stripes is identical to that of other Arab states which adopted similar flags to express the idea of a federation between them. Iraq's flag was designed in 1963 in response to a proposed union with Egypt and Syria, each of which already had identical flags, but with two green stars. The Iraqi flag was given three stars in anticipation of the union, but this failed to materialize. Iraq still flies this design as its flag, while the other two countries have replaced it.

Iraq   2:3

IRAN

The new version of the flag of Iran has been in use since July 1980. The white pattern along the edges of the green and white stripes is an inscription reading *Allah Akbar* (Allah is great) repeated 22 times. This represents the date when the Ayatollah Khomeini returned to Iran. In the centre of the flag is the new national emblem.

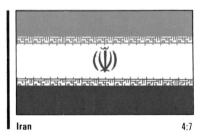

Iran   4:7

AFGHANISTAN

The latest national flag was adopted in 1980, but keeps the same colours as previous ones. In the canton is the new national emblem, which also has some traditional components, such as the pulpit and the sheaves of wheat. At the top is a rising sun and a red star, and at the bottom an open book, representing the Koran.

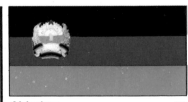

Afghanistan   1:2

Pakistan 2:3

Bangladesh 3:5

India 2:3

Sri Lanka 5:9

PAKISTAN

It is obvious from its national flag that Pakistan is a Muslim state. The traditional crescent moon and five-pointed star of Islam stand out large in white upon a plain green field, green being the traditional colour of Islam. However, the Hindus, Buddhists and Christians of Pakistan are represented in the flag by a vertical white stripe in the hoist. The design was based on the old Muslim League flag used after 1906 and was adopted when Pakistan gained independence from Britain in 1947.

BANGLADESH

A plain dark green flag with a large central red disc set slightly towards the hoist became the new flag of Bangladesh after it broke away from Pakistan in 1971. The green in the flag is said to represent the fertility of the land, while the red disc commemorates the blood shed in the struggle for freedom.

INDIA

The national flag of India evolved over several decades from designs used during the period when the country was trying to free itself from British rule. Mahatma Gandhi suggested the white stripe, and former spinning wheel emblem, which was altered on independence to a wheel called the *chakra*. This represents the dynamism of peaceful change. The three colours stand for courage and sacrifice (orange), truth and peace (white) and faith and chivalry (green). It became the national flag in 1947.

SRI LANKA

Sri Lanka has an unusual national flag. It is divided into two gold-bordered panels, the one nearer the hoist being narrower than the other. In this smaller panel are two vertical stripes representing the island's minority groups: green for Muslims, orange for the Hindu Tamils. The larger panel contains the royal flag of the old kingdom of Kandy, in the centre of the island, before the British captured it in 1815. The present flag was adopted in 1951, three years after the country gained its independence from Britain.

Maldive Islands 2:3

Nepal 4:3

MALDIVE ISLANDS
The thousand islands referred to in the local name for the Maldives have a national flag that records their long historical link with the religion of Islam. Like many other Muslim states in the Indian Ocean and on the Persian Gulf, the Maldives once flew a plain red flag. But early in the present century a plain green panel charged with a white crescent was added to the design. The latest flag, officially adopted in 1965 after the British left the islands, has a broad red border (a remnant from the old design) around the green panel.

NEPAL
The national flag of the Himalayan kingdom of Nepal has a unique shape. It originated when two separate triangular pennants of different shape were joined together in the 19th century. These were the flag of the royal family, with its emblem of a horizontal crescent moon, and below it the flag of the powerful Rana family, whose symbol was the sun. The latest version of this combined flag was officially adopted in 1962. The crescent and sun symbols appear in plain white on a crimson field, crimson being the national colour of Nepal. The entire flag has a narrow blue border. The flag is said to symbolize the hope that Nepal will last as long as the sun and moon.

BHUTAN
The name of this Himalayan state in the local Tibetan language means 'land of the dragon'. Accordingly the national flag has a fearsome representation of a wingless dragon prominently featured in black and white in the centre. The same word for dragon, *druk*, also means 'thunder', because it was a traditional belief that the thunder often heard in this mountainous country was the sound of roaring dragons among the high Himalayan peaks. The presence of the dragon in the flag may also be explained by Bhutan's historical links with China, whose emperors flew a golden yellow flag on which was a dragon. This association with China may also explain the yellow in the flag of Bhutan. The orange-red colour in the lower part of the flag symbolizes the Buddhist religion of the country and first appeared in the flag in the 1960s.

BURMA
Since it became independent from Britain in 1948, Burma has had a plain red flag with a dark blue canton charged with white symbols. The only change came in 1974, when the symbols in the canton were altered to represent the new socialist ideology of the country. A ring of 14 stars, one for each of Burma's states, now surrounds an emblem consisting of a gearwheel, representing industry, and a rice plant, symbolizing agriculture.

THAILAND
Thailand has a horizontally striped flag of red, white and blue known as the *Trairanga*, which it uses as the national, state and merchant flags. Each of the red and white stripes is one-sixth of the width of the flag, while the central blue stripe is one-third of the width.

Thailand has been known for centuries as the 'land of the white elephant'. According to legend, Zacca, the founder of the nation, passed through many transformations before finally becoming a white elephant. An elephant emblem still appears on the Thai naval ensign. Before 1916 it was also to be seen on the plain red national flag. In that year, the king noticed it being flown upside down in a village – a disrespectful error since the sacred elephant was seen with its legs pointing stiffly up at the sky. The outcome was a newly designed national flag that could not be hoisted upside down, a horizontally striped flag. A flag of red and white stripes was adopted for a brief time and then, in 1917, replaced with the present design.

LAOS

The national flag of Laos has three horizontal stripes of red, blue and red, with the central blue stripe twice as wide as each of the red ones. In the centre is a white disc, the diameter of which is four-fifths of the width of the blue stripe.

This design was the flag of the Communist political movement known as the Lao Patriotic Front, or Pathet Lao, which defeated government forces in the struggle for control of the country during the 1960s and 70s.

The flag of the former regime, the Kingdom of Laos, was plain red with a symbolic white emblem in the centre. This consisted of three elephants standing on a flight of stairs beneath a parasol. The parasol is a traditional symbol of royalty in Laos. According to legend, the founder of the country arrived there in about 1350 carrying a white parasol and riding on a white elephant. He united the separate warring states of the region to form the kingdom of Lan Xang (Land of the Million Elephants). The five steps in the emblem represented the five moral precepts of Theravada Buddhism, the religion of the Laotian people since ancient times.

Because the traditional values represented in its emblem did not reflect the ideology of the new Communist rulers, the old flag of Laos was replaced by the present design.

Bhutan   2:3

Thailand   2:3

Burma   5:9

Laos   2:3

KAMPUCHEA

Since 1975 Democratic Kampuchea (formerly Cambodia) has flown a plain red national flag. In the centre is an emblem comprising a yellow silhouette of the ancient temple at Angkor Wat. Although both the red colour of the flag and the Angkor Wat emblem are traditional symbols, used in all previous flags of the country, the People's Republic of Kampuchea adopted the latest form, which has five towers, in 1979.

VIETNAM

The simple design of the national flag of Vietnam – a five-pointed yellow (or gold) star on a red field – is basically the same as that flown by the forces who fought under Ho Chi-minh against the Japanese occupation of the country in World War II. It became the national flag of North Vietnam in 1945 after Emperor Bao Dai surrendered power to Ho Chi-minh. The shape of the star was slightly altered ten years later to create the flag still in use today. This flag is also flown in the territory formerly known as South Vietnam and now united with North Vietnam.

MALAYSIA

The federal structure of Malaysia is reflected in the design of its national flag, flown since 1963. The 13 states, with the capital territory of Kuala Lumpur, are represented by the 14 horizontal stripes in red and white in the fly. The blue canton recalls Malaysia's history as part of the old British Empire. In it are a crescent and star acknowledging that the national religion is Islam. Yellow, the colour of royalty, was chosen for these symbols to represent those states of Malaysia with sultans.

SINGAPORE

When Singapore broke away from the federation of Malaysia in 1963 to become an independent state, it retained its flag as its new national flag. Like many other flags in South-East Asia, its colours are red and white, arranged as two equal, horizontal stripes, red over white. In the upper hoist, in the red stripe, are a white crescent and a ring of five white stars. This emblem symbolizes the new nation setting out to achieve five ideals of democracy, peace, progress, justice and equality.

Kampuchea (Cambodia)   2:3

Malaysia   1:2

Vietnam   2:3

Singapore   2:3

Indonesia   2:3

INDONESIA
Indonesia's national flag is a simple bicolour of two equal, horizontal stripes, red over white. Its origin goes back to the Majapahit Empire, founded in the late 13th century, which flew a red and white flag. These colours were adopted by political groups in the 1920s and became established as the national flag in 1945, when Indonesia proclaimed its independence.

Papua New Guinea   3:4

PAPUA NEW GUINEA
When Papua New Guinea became independent from Australia in 1975, it adopted as its national flag a design which had been used to designate the country since 1971. It is halved diagonally from the head of the hoist to the foot of the fly. The lower half is black and is charged with the stars of the Southern Cross constellation in white. The upper half is red and bears a gold bird of paradise in flight.

BRUNEI
Since 1906 the national flag of Brunei has had a field of plain yellow which, as in the Malaysian flag, represents the royalty of the sultan. The field is divided diagonally from the head of the hoist to the foot of the fly by two parallel stripes, a broad white one above a narrower black one. In 1959 the red state emblem was added to the centre of the flag.

Brunei   1:2

THE PHILIPPINES
The Republic of the Philippines flies a national flag with two equal, horizontal stripes, blue over red. In the hoist is a white equilateral triangle bearing a large gold sun with eight rays representing the eight provinces of the Philippines that led the revolt against Spanish rule in 1898. Around the sun, in each corner of the triangle, are three smaller five-pointed stars. These represent the three main island groups of the Philippines. The flag is also used as the state and merchant flags and the naval ensign. When flown upside down, so that the red of courage and sacrifice is at the top, it becomes the war ensign, or army flag.

The Philippines flag was first designed in 1898, during Spanish rule, by exiles in Hong Kong and has been used as the national flag ever since.

Philippines   1:2

CHINA

Red, the colour symbolizing Communism, is also the traditional colour of the Chinese people and is appropriately the colour of their present national flag. In the upper hoist is a large five-pointed star, a symbol of the ideological programme of the Communist party of China, and to its right, an arc of four smaller stars representing the four main social classes of the Chinese people – workers, peasants, petty bourgeoisie and 'patriotic capitalists' – united under the leadership of the party. The five stars together also stand for the unity of China's principal traditional territories – China itself, Sinkiang, Mongolia, Manchuria and Tibet.

The number five has long had a symbolical significance in Chinese thought, and its use in the flag (also seen in the five points of the stars) reinforces the idea of national unity.

A red flag was used by the Chinese Communists from 1932, when the Chinese Soviet Republic was established in Kiangsi province. Its military flag was plain red with a gold star and a hammer and sickle emblem. The present design became the official national flag of China in 1949, when the Communist forces of Mao Tse-tung finally ousted the Nationalists led by Chiang Kai-shek.

TAIWAN

The flag of Taiwan has a plain red field and an emblem known as the 'White Sun in Blue Sky' in the canton. This emblem was the flag adopted in 1895 by Sun Yat-sen's Society for Regenerating China. In 1914, a red field was added to this emblem to create a war ensign for Sun Yat-sen's new Nationalist (Kuomintang) party. In 1928, this flag was adopted by the Nationalists as the national flag of China and was the flag of General Chiang Kai-shek's forces in the long struggle for control of China against Mao Tse-tung's Communist army.

After the final defeat of the Nationalists in 1949, Chiang Kai-shek and his forces moved to the island of Formosa, now called Taiwan, and set up the state of Nationalist China there. The old Nationalist flag of China thus became the flag of Taiwan.

China   2:3

Taiwan   2:3

Hong Kong   1:2

HONG KONG

A British dependent territory on the coast of China since 1841, Hong Kong has a distinguishing flag consisting of the British Blue Ensign (the flag used on state vessels) with the coat-of-arms of the colony inside a white roundel in the fly. The coat-of-arms dates from 1959. In the shield are two three-masted junks and above, in the chief, a naval crown. Gold crowned lions, symbolizing Britain, form the crest and the dexter supporter, while the sinister supporter is a gold dragon, representing China.

Mongolia 1:2

North Korea 1:2

MONGOLIA

The flag of the Mongolian People's Republic is basically a plain red flag of Communism, with a central vertical stripe in sky blue, the Mongolian national colour. The resulting design is, in fact, a tricolour of equal stripes of red, blue and red. In the upper hoist is the gold star of the Communist party, placed above the ancient traditional symbol of Mongolia, the *soyonbo*, which is illustrated and described on page 19. The two symbols together represent the ideology of Communism hand in hand with traditional Mongolian life and thought. The present flag was officially adopted in 1940.

NORTH KOREA

The Korean Democratic People's Republic, founded in 1948, has a flag of horizontal, blue, red and blue stripes separated by white fimbriations. In the red stripe, set towards the hoist, is a white disc charged with the red star of the Communist party.

SOUTH KOREA

White, the traditional colour of the Korean people, appears in the national flag of the Republic of Korea, where it also expresses the desire for peace. In the centre of the flag is a disc halved by an S-shaped line, the upper half being red and the lower half blue. This is based on the ancient Chinese Yin-Yang symbol, which represents all the opposites that occur in nature, such as male–female, good–evil, and so on. In the corners of the flag are four trigrams, each one representing one of the four seasons and cardinal points and one of the elements of the universe – the earth, moon, sun and heaven.

The present flag, adopted in 1950, was based on a design of 1882.

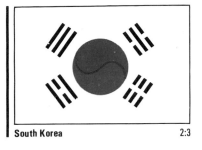

South Korea 2:3

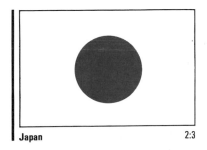

Japan 2:3

JAPAN

The geographical position of Japan in the East is expressed both in the name of the country, Nihon-Koku (Land of the Rising Sun) and in the national flag, known as the 'Sun Disc'. The simple, beautiful design of this flag consists of a large red disc in the centre of a plain white field. Flags with such sun discs have been used by emperors and warriors in Japan for many centuries, and in 1872 the present design was officially approved as the national flag. A sun disc with 16 radiating rays is used as the Japanese naval ensign.

FLAGS OF AUSTRALIA
AND OCEANIA

American Samoa

Western Samoa

Cook Islands

Tonga
Niue

Northern Marianas

Guam
Pitcairn Islands

Marshall Islands

Caroline Islands

Kiribati

Nauru

Tuvalu

Solomon Islands

Vanuatu
Fiji

Northern
Territory
Queensland

Western Australia

New South Wales

South Australia

Victoria

Tasmania

New Zealand

Australia   1:2

New South Wales   1:2

AUSTRALIA

Australia's historical origin as an over-seas colony of Britain is reflected in its national flag. The basis of the design is the British Blue Ensign, with the addition of the five stars of the Southern Cross constellation in the fly and a larger star known as the 'Commonwealth Star' below the canton. The seven points of this star represent Australia's six states and one territory. This flag, flown since 1909, is also used in Australia's dependencies.

The emblems on the state and territorial flags are as follows:

NEW SOUTH WALES

A St George's cross charged with a lion in the centre and an eight-pointed star on each arm.

QUEENSLAND

A blue Maltese cross on a white field, with a royal crown at the centre.

SOUTH AUSTRALIA

A white-backed piping shrike, or Murray magpie on a yellow field.

TASMANIA

The red lion from the crest of the state arms on a white field.

VICTORIA

Five stars of the Southern Cross constellation surmounted by a crown.

WESTERN AUSTRALIA

The black swan native to Western Australia on a yellow field.

NORTHERN TERRITORY

The Southern Cross in the hoist and the desert rose in the ochre fly.

Queensland   1:2

South Australia   1:2

Tasmania   1:2

Victoria   1:2

Northern Territory   1:2

Western Australia   1:2

New Zealand 1:2

Guam 21:40

Nauru 1:2

Kiribati 10:17

Solomon Islands 1:2

NEW ZEALAND
Like Australia, New Zealand flies a national flag based on the design of the British Blue Ensign. It also incorporates the Southern Cross constellation in the fly, but includes only four of the stars. These are coloured red and fimbriated in white. The flag was adopted in 1902.

GUAM
Guam has been a dependency of the United States since 1898 and flies its flag only with the American 'Stars and Stripes'. Its flag is of plain blue with a red border. In the centre, edged in red, is a shield-shaped scene of a beach with a coconut palm and, offshore, an outrigger canoe. Across the scene the name 'Guam' appears in red capital letters. The flag dates from 1917.

NAURU
The flag of the tiny Pacific island of Nauru is unusual in that it is a diagrammatic map of the island's location in the sea just south of the equator. It is a simple, but ingenious design resulting from a competition to find a new flag for the island nation on independence in 1968. The 12 points of the star represent the island's tribes.

KIRIBATI
Formerly the Gilbert Islands, this newly-independent state flies a flag which is made up from the shield of its coat of arms. This was adopted in 1979.

TUVALU
On independence from Britain in 1978, Tuvalu, once known as the Ellice Islands, adopted a pale blue flag with a Union Flag in the canton and, in the fly, a pattern of nine yellow five-pointed stars representing the geographical position of the nine main islands.

Tuvalu 1:2

SOLOMON ISLANDS
In 1978 the Solomon Islands became independent from Britain and adopted a new flag. The five white five-pointed stars in the upper hoist represent the five main islands of the South Pacific group.

PITCAIRN ISLANDS
A flag for local use was granted to Pitcairn in 1984. It is the British Blue Ensign with the whole arms in the fly.

NORTHERN MARIANAS
The sea-blue flag of this island group has a white star surmounting a grey *latte* stone, which represents the old traditions of the Chamorro people. Adopted in 1976.

AMERICAN SAMOA
This group of islands is an American dependency with its own constitution. The present flag was adopted in 1960. Inside a white triangle, an American eagle in proper colours holds a Samoan chief's staff and ceremonial knife, representing American protection of the Samoan people.

WESTERN SAMOA
Western Samoa, a group of South Pacific islands, has had a national flag since 1948, 14 years before it became an independent state. In addition to blue, its colours are the traditional red and white used in Samoan flags in the 19th century. The design links Samoa with other nations of the southern hemisphere by its inclusion of the Southern Cross constellation. This appears as five white stars in a blue canton. The rest of the flag is plain red.

VANUATU
Formerly the New Hebrides, this state became independent in 1980. The flag has a black triangle with a boar's tusk in yellow, inside which are two crossed fern leaves.

American Samoa   1:2

Pitcairn Islands   1:2

Western Samoa   1:2

Northern Marianas   2:3

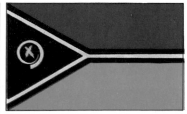
Vanuatu   11:18

FIJI
Fiji's flag shows the island's link with the United Kingdom. The shield in the fly is from Fiji's state coat of arms, and dates from 1980.

TONGA
The red cross in the fly of the Tongan flag, similar to the methodist badge and the Red Cross flag, illustrates the Tongan's adherence to the Christian religion. .

NIUE
A semi-independent depenency of New Zealand, Niue adopted its own flag in 1974.

COOK ISLANDS
The fifteen stars in the fly of the Cook Islands' flag represent the fifteen islands of the group.

MICRONESIA
This flag is based on that of the United Nations, since Micronesia is a trust territory. The four stars stand for the four states, and the flag was adopted in 1978. The former parts of Micronesia are now separate and self-governing, and have flags of their own. These are Belau and the Marshall Islands. The disk in the flag of Belau represents the moon.

Niue   1:2

Cook Islands   1:2

Micronesia   10:19

Fiji   1:2

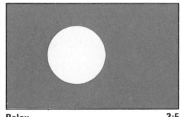
Belau   3:5

Tonga   1:2

Marshall Islands   10:19

FLAGS OF AFRICA

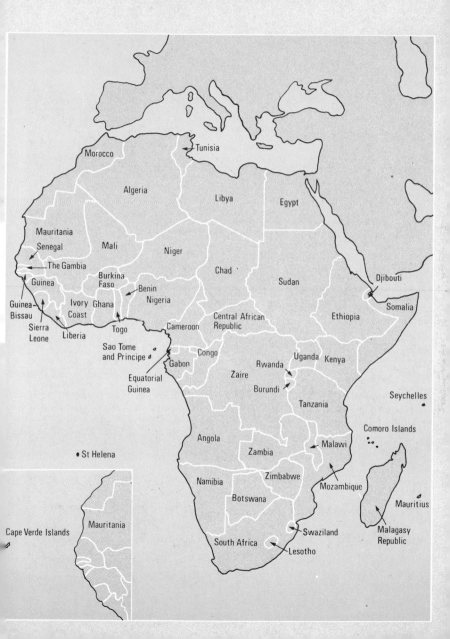

SUDAN

The design and colours of the national flag flown in Sudan since 1969 identify the country as a state with close ties with the Arab world. The flag is basically a tricolour of equal, horizontal stripes in red, white and black with a green triangle in the hoist. These are the colours to be found in the flags of several other Arab states today.

The design of the flag is based on the Arab revolt flag used in Syria, Iraq and Jordan after 1918. The colours of this flag are still to be seen in the present Sudanese flag, but arranged differently to resemble other Arab flags adopted since 1958.

EGYPT

The current flag of Egypt, which dates in its present form from 1984, is very similar to the one used by the movement which overthrew the monarchy in 1952 and which popularised the red, white and black colours which have since been adopted by several other Arab states. They were first used on the national flag in 1958, when Egypt was united with Syria in the United Arab Republic. At that time the flag had two green stars in the centre representing the two countries, and is still to be seen in the flag of Syria. That union was disolved in 1961, but Egypt continued to use its flag until 1972. In that year, Egypt, Syria and Libya joined the Federation of Arab Republics, which had a common flag in the same colours with a gold hawk in the centre. Although the federation did not survive the withdrawal of Libya in 1977, and later of Syria, Egypt continued to use its flag until 1984, when the gold hawk was replaced by the present gold eagle.

The emblem of the gold hawk on the old flag symbolised the tribe of the prophet Mohammed. On the new flag, the gold eagle emblem symbolises the Arab hero Saladin. It is all in gold, including the breast shield. Beneath the eagle, the scroll contains the country's title: Egyptian Arab Republic. The Egyptian president's flag has the eagle emblem repeated in the upper hoist.

LIBYA

Until late 1977 the Libyan Arab Republic flew the flag of the Federation of Arab Republics as its national flag. In protest against the visit of Egypt's President Sadat to Israel in 1977, Libya left the federation and ceased to use its flag. Now it has a plain green flag, symbolizing Colonel Ghaddafi's concept of the 'Green Revolution'.

TUNISIA

The national flag of Tunisia is red with a central white roundel containing a red crescent and star, the traditional symbols of the Muslim religion. The flag originated in about 1835, when the country was still officially under Turkish rule. To avoid undesirable repercussions while giving Tunisia some local identity, a flag that was closely similar to the Turkish flag was created. This flag survived even a period of French rule and became adopted as the national flag on independence in 1956.

ALGERIA

The traditional green, white and red colours of Islam also appear in the national flag adopted by the Algerian Democratic People's Republic on its independence from France in 1962. The flag is halved vertically, with green next to the hoist and white in the fly. Over the dividing line is the red star and crescent of Islam.

The present flag is said to date from a design created by an Algerian patriot who fought against French colonisers in the early 19th century. But a flag designed for an Algerian Muslim political movement in 1928 is a more probable origin. This flag was adopted by the liberation movement that fought against French rule after 1954 and was adopted as the national flag on independence in 1962.

MOROCCO

The present national flag of Morocco dates from 1915, although the country did not gain its independence from French and Spanish rule until 1956. The flag has the plain red field used by the country's ruling dynasty for the past three centuries. In the centre is a star-shaped pentagram, or Solomon's Seal emblem, in green.

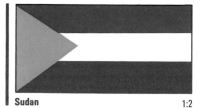

Sudan 1:2

Tunisia 2:3

Egypt 2:3

Algeria 2:3

Libya 2:3

Morocco 2:3

MAURITANIA

The Muslim religion practised by the majority of the Mauritanian people is reflected both in the official name of the country – the Mauritanian Islamic Republic – and in the national flag. This is a plain emerald green flag with a gold crescent and star in the centre. Green and gold are also two of the colours of pan-African flags used by black nations to the south. The present flag was adopted in 1959, just prior to independence from France in 1960.

Mauritania 2:3

SENEGAL
The national flag of the Republic of Senegal is a vertical tricolour of green, yellow and red stripes. In the centre is a green five-pointed star symbolizing the Muslim faith of the majority of the population. This flag was adopted in 1960 when Senegal gained independence from France. The new state, Senegambia, is a confederation set up in 1981 by the Gambia and Senegal. Both states still use their own flags as before.

Senegal   2:3

GUINEA-BISSAU
The pan-African colours of red, yellow and green appear in the national flag adopted by the Republic of Guinea-Bissau on independence from Portugal in 1973. A red vertical stripe appears in the hoist, with two equal, horizontal stripes, yellow above green, in the fly. On the red stripe is a black five-pointed star representing the PAIGC political party that led the independence struggle from 1962.

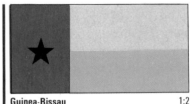

Guinea-Bissau   1:2

GUINEA
As a former French colony, the Republic of Guinea adopted a national flag based on the design of the French tricolour when the country became independent in 1958. The colours used, however, were those of pan-African unity: red, yellow and green. They also represent symbolically the three words of Guinea's national motto: work (red), justice (yellow) and solidarity (green).

MALI
The national flag of Mali is a vertical tricolour with equal stripes of green, yellow and red. Its design is based on the tricolour of France, of which Mali was a colony until independence in 1960. The colours are those of pan-African unity.

Guinea   2:3

THE GAMBIA
The Republic of The Gambia has a national flag consisting of five horizontal stripes of red, white, blue, white and green. The blue stripe represents the Gambia River that flows through the country, while the red stripe stands for the sun and the green for agriculture. The flag was adopted in 1965 on independence from Britain.

Mali   2:3

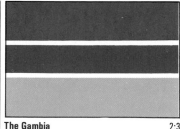
The Gambia   2:3

Sierra Leone   2:3

SIERRA LEONE
On independence from Britain in 1961, Sierra Leone adopted a national flag with equal, horizontal stripes in green, white and blue. The green stands for the nation's agriculture, white for peace and blue for the ocean.

LIBERIA
At first glance, the national flag of Liberia may appear similar to the flag of the United States. The Liberian flag has 11 horizontal stripes alternating in red and white in the fly, and a white five-pointed star in the blue canton.

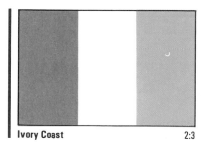
Liberia   10:19

Liberia was founded in about 1821 as an American colony for freed black slaves who wished to return to Africa from the United States. From 1827 the colony had its own flag based on the American 'Stars and Stripes' and this was the basis for the new flag designed by a group of women for the colony's independence in 1847. This is still flown today.

IVORY COAST
As a former colony of France, the Ivory Coast adopted a flag based on the design of the French tricolour when it gained independence in 1960. The colours are symbolic. Orange stands for the northern savannas, white for peace and unity, and green for the forests.

Ivory Coast   2:3

BURKINA FASO
Formerly Upper Volta, this country adopted a new name and flag in 1984, replacing those used since independence in 1960. The flag is composed of two red and green horizontal stripes, superimposed with a gold star. The colours are the pan-African colours of Burkina Faso's neighbours.

Burkina Faso   2:3

GHANA

A horizontal tricolour of equal stripes in red, yellow and green, with a black star symbolizing liberty in the centre, was adopted as the national flag of Ghana on independence from Britain in 1957. The colours were those of the flag hoisted in 1894 by Ethiopia, Africa's oldest independent nation and, following Ghana's lead, were adopted by other former colonies as a symbol of Black pan-African unity.

Ghana   2:3

Togo   3:5

TOGO

Since gaining independence from France in 1960, the Togo Republic has flown a national flag in the pan-African colours of red, yellow and green. The green and yellow form five alternating horizontal stripes in the fly, while the red appears as a canton containing a large white five-pointed star. The green is said to symbolize Togo's agriculture and hope for future prosperity; the yellow stands for the country's mineral wealth and faith in the value of work; and the red represents virtuous sacrifice and the blood shed in the struggle for independence. The white star is a symbol of national purity.

BENIN

The red, yellow and green pan-African colours appeared in the national flag adopted by Benin (then called Dahomey) in 1959 prior to independence from France the following year. However, in 1975, the country became the People's Republic of Benin and adopted a new flag. This is plain green with a large five-pointed star in red in the upper hoist.

NIGER

The national flag adopted by the Republic of Niger just before independence from France in 1960 is a horizontal tricolour of orange, white and green stripes. In the centre is an orange disc representing the sun. The colours in the stripes are also significant. Orange stands for the Sahara desert, in the north, white for goodness and purity, and green for the grasslands in the south.

Benin   2:3

Niger   6:7

NIGERIA

Nigeria's national flag is a vertical tricolour of green, white and green stripes. The design was chosen in 1959 after a competition to find a new national flag in time for Nigeria's independence from Britain in 1960. The designer of the flag is said to have been so impressed by his country's forests as he flew over them that he decided to use green as the basis of his design.

CHAD

The vertical stripes of the French tricolour inspired the design adopted by this former French colony for its national flag in 1959. The colours – blue, yellow and red – are a compromise between the blue, white and red of the French flag and the green, yellow and red pan-African colours. The blue is said to represent the sky, the streams of the south, and hope. Yellow stands for the sun and the Sahara desert in the north, and red represents national sacrifice.

CENTRAL AFRICAN REPUBLIC

The national flag of the Central African Republic, adopted in 1958, combines the green, yellow and red of pan-African unity with the blue, white and red of the flag of the country's former colonial ruler, France. The colours are arranged as equal, horizontal stripes of blue, white, green and yellow, with a vertical red stripe down the centre. In the upper hoist is a yellow star symbolizing liberty. The flag expresses symbolically the need for friendship between European and African nations, which are united by the common blood of mankind.

CAMEROON

Like many other former African colonies, the United Republic of Cameroon flies a national flag in the pan-African colours. They are arranged as a vertical tricolour, with a green stripe nearest the hoist. In the central red stripe is a yellow star of liberty. The present design dates from 1975 and differs only slightly from the original tricolour adopted in 1957 before independence from France in 1960.

Chad   2:3

Central African Republic   3:5

Nigeria   1:2

Cameroon   2:3

EQUATORIAL GUINEA

The national flag of the Republic of Equatorial Guinea has three horizontal stripes in green, white and red, with a blue triangle in the hoist. The green represents the natural wealth of the country; white stands for peace, and red for the nation's struggle for independence from Spanish colonial rule. The blue symbolizes the sea that surrounds the country's offshore islands. The state flag bears the state coat-of-arms in the centre. Both flags were officially adopted on independence in 1968.

Equatorial Guinea   5:8

GABON

A simple horizontal tricolour of green, yellow and blue stripes was adopted as Gabon's national flag on independence from France in 1960. The green represents Gabon's thick forests, the source of a large proportion of the nation's wealth. The yellow stripe was formerly a thinner line representing the equator, on which Gabon lies, and can now be interpreted as symbolizing the sun. The blue stands for the sea.

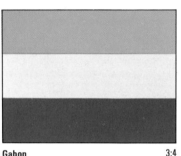

Gabon   3:4

Congo   2:3

CONGO

The socialist ideology of the People's Republic of the Congo is clearly proclaimed in the national flag the country has flown since the last day of 1969. It is a plain red flag with an emblem in the upper hoist containing typical symbols of socialism: a gold five-pointed star above a hammer crossed with a hoe. On either side of the emblem is a palm branch symbolizing peace. The colours of the Congo's flag are the pan-African colours adopted by several other former colonies in the continent.

ZAIRE

The pan-African colours of red, yellow and green appear in the national flag used by Zaire since 1971. The flag is green with a yellow disc in the centre in which appears an arm holding a blazing torch. This central emblem symbolizes the revolutionary spirit of the nation and was used by the Popular Movement of the Revolution formed in 1967 by President Joseph Mobutu.

Zaire   2:3

RWANDA

A simple vertical tricolour of red, yellow and green stripes with a large capital letter 'R' in the central yellow stripe is the national flag of the tiny Republic of Rwanda. The tricolour design dates from 1961, but because the flag was identical to that of Guinea, the letter 'R' was added later that year. The symbolism of the pan-African colours is as follows: red for the blood shed in the revolution that erupted in 1959; yellow for victory over tyranny; and green for hope for the future.

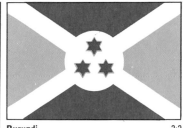

Rwanda 2:3

BURUNDI

The national flag of the Republic of Burundi is unique in its design. It is quartered by a white saltire. The top and bottom quarters are red, while the quarters in the hoist and fly are green. In the centre is a white disc containing three red six-pointed stars fimbriated in green. These stand for the three words in the national motto: Unity, Work, Progress.

Burundi 2:3

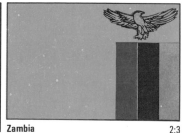

Angola 1:2

ANGOLA

The flag used by the Popular Movement for the Liberation of Angola (PMLA) during the struggle for independence from Portugal became the basis of the national flag flown in areas controlled by the party from 1975. It has two equal, horizontal stripes, red over black. In the centre is an emblem representing the country's socialist ideology. It consists of a yellow five-pointed star, and a half gearwheel crossed with a machete.

ZAMBIA

Zambia's national flag has an unusual design. It is plain green with three vertical stripes in red, black and orange in the fly. Above the stripes is a flying eagle, symbolizing freedom, in natural colours. The flag was officially adopted on independence from Britain in 1964. Its colours were derived from the flag used by the United Nationalist Independence Party (UNIP), which led the struggle for independence.

Zambia 2:3

ZIMBABWE

The new flag of Zimbabwe, adopted when legal independence was secured in 1980, is based on the colours of the ruling Patriotic Front, except for the white triangle. On this is placed the Zimbabwe Bird, a symbol used for a long time in Rhodesia, derived from carvings found in the ruined city of Zimbabwe. Behind this is placed a red star to symbolize the socialist policy of the new state.

MOZAMBIQUE

The flag of Mozambique displays the colours of FRELIMO, the nationlist movement which secured the country's independence from Portugal in 1975. The first national flag had the colours arranged in rays emerging from the upper hoist canton, but the present one, adopted in May 1983, is much like that of FRELIMO. The badge in the triangle is a simplified version of the national emblem.

MALAWI

The three horizontal stripes of black, red and green in the present national flag of Malawi were also in the flag adopted by the Malawi Congress Party in 1953. When the country became independent from Britain 11 years later, the symbol of the red rising sun was added to the black stripe to represent the beginning of a new era for Africa. This design was then adopted as Malawi's national flag.

BOTSWANA

The national flag of the Republic of Botswana is light blue with a horizontal black stripe fimbriated in white across the centre. The flag was officially adopted on independence from Britain in 1966. Its colours have a symbolical significance. The black and white stripes, inspired by the zebra's markings, express Botswana's commitment to a nation based on equality between the different races. The pale blue symbolizes the rainwater so essential for the survival of the nation's important cattle industry.

Zimbabwe 13:25

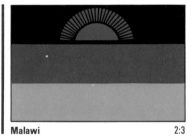

Malawi 2:3

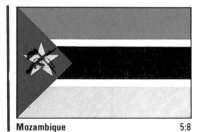

Mozambique 5:8

Botswana 2:3

NAMIBIA

At present, Namibia remains under the control of South Africa, despite calls by the United Nations Organization to grant the territory independence. The local political organization SWAPO has led the internal struggle for freedom from South African rule. It uses a flag with horizontal stripes of blue, red and green, and this may form the basis of Namibia's national flag when independence is finally achieved. Meanwhile, flags designed by the South African authorities are flown as well as the South African national flag.

LESOTHO

The traditional woven straw hat worn by the people of Lesotho appears as a large white emblem on the national flag flown in the country since independence from Britain in 1966. The hat appears against a pale blue field representing rain. In the hoist are two narrow, vertical stripes in green and red standing, respectively, for the land and faith in the future.

SWAZILAND

Since independence from Britain in 1967, the Kingdom of Swaziland has flown a distinctive national flag. It can best be described as having a blue field, with a broad horizontal stripe in crimson across the centre and fimbriated with two narrow yellow stripes. The crimson stripe bears a charge consisting of the traditional weapons of an Emasotsha warrior: an oxhide shield, two assegai and a fighting stick.

SOUTH AFRICA

The flag of the Dutch Prince of Orange brought to South Africa by the first Dutch settlers in the 17th century, forms the basis of South Africa's national flag flown since 1928. It is a horizontal tricolour of orange, white and blue stripes. The centre of the white stripe is charged with the flags of the former Dutch republics of the Orange Free State and the Transvaal, with the British Union Flag on their left. The Orange Free State flag is placed in a vertical position between the other two.

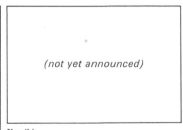

(not yet announced)

Namibia

Swaziland 2:3

Lesotho 2:3

South Africa 2:3

MALAGASY REPUBLIC

Red, white and green are the colours of the national flag adopted in 1958 by the Malagasy Republic on the island of Madagascar. They are arranged as two horizontal stripes, red over green, with a broad vertical white stripe in the hoist. The red stands for sovereignty, white for purity, and green for hope. Red and white were also the colours of historical flags of South-East Asia, from where Madagascar's first people came before AD 1000, and of later flags used on the island.

Malagasy Republic   2:3

Tanzania   2:3

Uganda   2:3

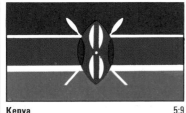

Kenya   5:9

TANZANIA

When Tanzania united with the island of Zanzibar in 1964 to form the United Republic of Tanzania, a new flag was adopted that included elements from the flags of both regions. It has a broad black stripe fimbriated in yellow running diagonally from the lower hoist to the upper fly. The rest of the flag is green above the stripe and blue below it.

UGANDA

On independence from Britain in 1962, Uganda hoisted an official flag in the black, yellow and red colours of the Uganda People's Congress, which had just won the national election. The black stands for the African people, yellow for the sun, and red for the brotherhood of man. The colours are arranged as six equal, horizontal stripes in a repeated sequence of black, yellow and red. In the centre is a white disc charged with a crested crane in natural colours.

KENYA

The Kenyan national flag has three equal, horizontal stripes in black, red and green separated by narrow fimbriations in white. In the centre is an emblem consisting of a Masai warrior's shield with two crossed spears. The black stripe stands for the African people; the red for the blood common to all races; and the green for the fertile land of Kenya. The design was based on the flag of the Kenya African National Union (KANU), which led the struggle for independence from Britain. The present flag dates from 1963, when independence was achieved.

Cape Verde Islands   2:3

CAPE VERDE ISLANDS
On independence from Portugal in 1975, the Cape Verde Islands adopted a national flag in the pan-African colours used by other former African colonies. It has two equal, horizontal stripes, yellow over green, in the fly, with a vertical red stripe in the hoist. In the upper part of the red stripe is an emblem comprising a five-pointed black star positioned above a yellow seashell surrounded by a garland of maize leaves and two corn cobs.

SOMALIA
The national flag of the Somali Democratic Republic dates from 1954. It was then the flag of the southern part of the country, at that time a separate country administered by Italy under mandate from the United Nations and known as Somalia. When the colony of British Somaliland, to the north, united with Somalia in 1960 to form present-day Somalia, the flag of the southern region was adopted as the national flag of the new country. Inspired by the United Nations flag, it is light blue and has a five-pointed white star in the centre. The points represent the five areas of East Africa where Somalis live: the two regions of Somalia, northern Kenya, Jibuti and southern Ethiopia.

Somalia   2:3

DJIBOUTI
On independence from France in 1977, Djibouti adopted a national flag with two horizontal stripes, light blue above light green, with a white triangle in the hoist. Inside the triangle is a five-pointed red star.

Djibouti   2:3

ETHIOPIA
The Socialist Republic of Ethiopia flies as its national flag a horizontal tricolour of equal stripes in green, yellow and red. These colours were first used as a national flag towards the end of the 19th century, when they appeared as three separate pennants which were flown together, one above the other. A single, rectangular flag was designed in 1897 with the red stripe at the top, the green at the bottom. The present arrangement of stripes has been in continuous use since 1941.

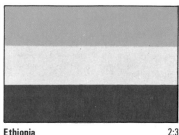

Ethiopia   2:3

ST HELENA

The British dependent territory of St Helena, with its dependencies of Ascension Island and the Tristan da Cunha group, flies the British Blue Ensign with the territory's ornately framed badge in the fly. This portrays a sailing ship between two sea cliffs. A more distinctive local flag is under consideration.

St Helena   1:2

SÃO TOMÉ AND PRINCIPE

On independence from Portugal in 1975, these two islands hoisted a horizontal tricolour of green, yellow and green stripes, with a red triangle in the hoist. On the yellow stripe are two five-pointed black stars representing the two islands.

Sao Tome and Principe   1:2

COMORO ISLANDS

Since 1975 when they declared their independence from France the Comoro Islands have flown a flag with a crescent and four white stars. These represent their Muslim faith, and the four islands. The latest design adopted in 1978 has the crescent and stars on a plain green field.

MAURITIUS

Four equal, horizontal stripes in red, dark blue, yellow and green form the national flag adopted by the island of Mauritius on independence from Britain in 1968. Red stands for the struggle for independence, blue for the Indian Ocean, yellow for the golden future after independence and green for the lush vegetation of the island.

SEYCHELLES

In 1977, after a change of government, the Seychelles adopted a new flag that suggests the Indian Ocean surrounding the islands of the group. At the bottom of the flag is a dark green horizontal stripe, which is separated from the red upper part by a narrow, wavy white stripe.

Comoro Islands   3:5

Mauritius   2:3

Seychelles   1:2

FLAGS OF NORTH AND CENTRAL AMERICA

Virgin Islands (UK admin.)
Virgin Islands (US admin.)
St Christopher Nevis
Anguilla
Antigua
Montserrat
Dominica
St Lucia
St Vincent
Barbados
Grenada

Alaska

The Yukon

North West Territories

British Columbia

Alberta

Sask

Manitoba

Ontario

Quebec

Newfoundland

Prince Edward Island

Nova Scotia

New Brunswick

Me

Vt N H

Mas

N Y

R I

Conn

Penn

N J

Del

Ohio

DC

Md

W Va

Va

Wash

Oreg

Id

Mont

N Dak

Minn

Wis

Mich

S Dak

Wyo

Nev

Iowa

Neb

Ill

Ind

Ky

Utah

Col

Ks

Mo

N C

Calif

Tenn

S C

Ariz

N Mex

Okla

Ark

Mi

Ala

Geo

Texas

La

Flor

Hawaii

Mexico

Bahamas

Turks and Caicos Islands

Cuba

Dominican Republic

Cayman Islands

Haiti

Puerto Rico

Jamaica

Belize

Honduras

Guatemala

El Salvador

Nicaragua

Costa Rica

Panama

Netherlands Antilles

Canada   1:2

ALBERTA
An ultramarine blue flag with the shield from the province's arms in the centre. Adopted 1967.

BRITISH COLUMBIA
The banner of the province's arms, adopted 1960.

MANITOBA
The British Red Ensign with the shield of the province's arms in the fly. Adopted 1966.

NEW BRUNSWICK
The banner of the province's arms, adopted 1965.

NEWFOUNDLAND
This new design was adopted in 1980.

CANADA
After many years of discussion about the design of a new flag, Canada adopted the present design in 1965. It is a red flag, with a white square the full width of the flag in the centre. In the square is a large red maple leaf, Canada's national emblem.

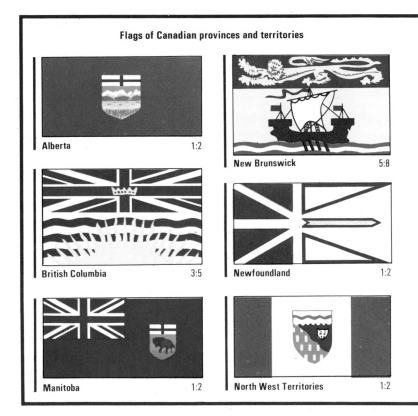

Flags of Canadian provinces and territories

Alberta   1:2

New Brunswick   5:8

British Columbia   3:5

Newfoundland   1:2

Manitoba   1:2

North West Territories   1:2

NORTH-WEST TERRITORIES
A blue flag, with a white square the full width of the flag in the centre, charged with the shield from the province's arms. Adopted 1969.

NOVA SCOTIA
A blue St Andrew's cross on a white field, with the Royal Arms of Scotland in the centre. Adopted 1929.

ONTARIO
The British Red Ensign, with the shield of the province's arms in the fly. Adopted 1965.

PRINCE EDWARD ISLAND
The banner of the province's arms, with a decorative red and white border. Adopted 1964.

QUEBEC
A white St George's cross on a blue field. In each quarter, a white French *fleur-de-lis*. Adopted 1948.

SASKATCHEWAN
A bicolour of horizontal stripes, green over yellow, with the shield of the province's arms in the upper hoist. In the fly, a prairie lily, the provincial emblem. Adopted 1969.

THE YUKON
A vertical tricolour of green, white and light blue stripes, with the full arms of the territory in the centre. The colours have a symbolical purpose. Green stands for The Yukon's forests, white for its snow, and blue for its lakes. Adopted 1968.

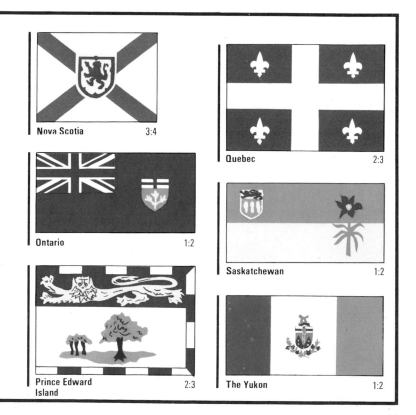

Nova Scotia   3:4

Ontario   1:2

Prince Edward Island   2:3

Quebec   2:3

Saskatchewan   1:2

The Yukon   1:2

United States 10:19

THE UNITED STATES

The 'Star-spangled Banner', the 'Stars and Stripes' and 'Old Glory' are the affectionate names given by Americans to their national flag. The flag has had the same basic design since 1777, during the War of Independence. It has 13 horizontal stripes, arranged as seven red stripes alternating with six white ones. They represent the original 13 colonies that rebelled against British rule in 1775 and they first appeared in the flag in that year. In addition to the stripes, 50 white five-pointed stars, representing the 50 states of the Union, appear on a dark blue field in the canton. They are arranged as five rows of six stars alternating with four rows of five stars. They first appeared in the flag in 1777, but then numbered only 13 to represent the rebelling colonies.

THE STATES OF THE UNION

The flags of the 50 states and the District of Columbia are described in alphabetical order.

ALABAMA

Although its official description is 'a crimson cross of St Andrew on a white field', the flag of Alabama is said to have originated in the Battle Flag flown by the southern states during the Civil War. Adopted 1895.

ALASKA

Alaska chose the design of its flag in 1927, 32 years before joining the Union. Designed by a 13-year-old schoolboy, it was selected out of 142 entries in a competition. Appropriately for the most northerly state in the Union, the flag depicts, in gold, the Great Bear constellation and the Pole Star on a dark blue field.

ARIZONA

The traditional red and yellow colours of Spain, which once ruled the area, and the blue and yellow colours of Arizona are combined in the state flag adopted in 1917. The central star represents Arizona's rich copper mines.

ARKANSAS

Arkansas flies a red flag containing a white lozenge with a blue border. Inside the lozenge is the name of the state and, below it, three blue stars representing the three countries which have ruled the state: Spain, France and the United States. Above the name is another blue star indicating that Arkansas was one of the southern states in the Civil War. In the blue border are 25 white stars to denote that Arkansas was the 25th state to join the Union. Adopted 1924.

CALIFORNIA

The present flag of California dates from 1846, when it was the flag of the Republic of California which had broken away from Mexico. The single star and one stripe were included in the design to show that the people wished to join the United States.

COLORADO

A strikingly modern design of 1911, the flag of Colorado is a horizontal tricolour of blue, white and blue stripes, with a central emblem consisting of a red letter 'C' around a yellow disc. The blue stands for the state's blue skies, white for its snow-covered peaks, and the yellow disc for its brilliant and abundant sunshine.

CONNECTICUT

The flag of Connecticut, adopted in 1897, has the state coat-of-arms on a blue field. Inside the ornate shield, on a white field, are three vines representing the three colonies that later formed the state.

DELAWARE

As the first state to ratify the constitution, Delaware proudly displays the date 'December 7, 1787' on its flag. The design consists of the state coat-of-arms on a buff lozenge in a blue field. Adopted 1913.

STATE FLAGS

The flags of the 50 states display a wide variety of designs. A large number bear the state seal or some other emblem of local significance upon a blue field. The flags of New Mexico and Colorado have a strikingly modern appearance, while that of Maryland reveals a purely heraldic design. Other flags recall historical links with France before the Louisiana Purchase of 1803 or membership of the Confederacy of southern states in the Civil War of 1861–5.

Arkansas   2:3

California   2:3

Colorado   2:3

Connecticut   26:33

Delaware   3:4

Alabama   1:1

Alaska   125:177

Arizona   2:3

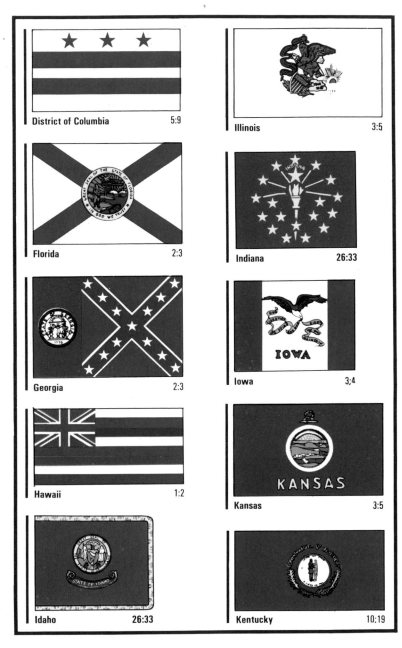

District of Columbia 5:9

Illinois 3:5

Florida 2:3

Indiana 26:33

Georgia 2:3

Iowa 3;4

Hawaii 1:2

Kansas 3:5

Idaho 26:33

Kentucky 10:19

DISTRICT OF COLUMBIA

Although not a state, the District of Columbia is unique in that it has within its boundaries the federal capital of the United States: the city of Washington, named after the nation's first president. The flag of the district is appropriately derived from the coat-of-arms of the Washington family. Adopted in 1938, the design has two horizontal red stripes surmounted by three five-pointed red stars, all on a white field.

FLORIDA

Florida's flag, like that of Alabama, has a red saltire on a white field, a design based on the Battle Flag used by the southern states in the Civil War. In the centre is the state seal containing a landscape in which an Indian woman is seen scattering flowers. Adopted 1900.

GEORGIA

The present striking design of Georgia's flag dates only from 1956, but was originally adopted in 1879. In the fly is the Battle Flag used in the Civil War by the southern states. In the hoist is a vertical blue stripe containing the state seal, which symbolizes the three branches of government that uphold the constitution.

HAWAII

In 1959 Hawaii became the 50th state to join the Union. Its flag, however, has a history going back to the 18th century. There are many stories to explain the presence of the British Union Flag in the canton, for Hawaii was never a British possession. According to one account, a Union Flag was presented to the king by the explorer George Vancouver in 1793 and flown over the royal palace. Stripes were introduced in a new design of about 1816, and the present flag dates from 1845.

IDAHO

The plain blue flag of Idaho, adopted in 1927, bears the state seal in the centre. It has a shield containing a mountain landscape; two supporters, a woman with a spear and scales and a miner holding a pick; and a crest with a moose's head and a Latin motto meaning 'May she endure forever'.

ILLINOIS

The plain white flag of Illinois, adopted in 1970, has an interesting central emblem. An eagle with outstretched wings is perched on a rock in a landscape. It holds a red scroll in its beak and a shield in its talons. The scroll bears the words 'State Sovereignty, National Union'. The shield has 13 white stars on a blue field in the chief and, in the base, 13 red and white vertical stripes. These represent the original colonies.

INDIANA

Indiana's plain blue flag bears a circular arrangement of stars and a blazing torch in gold. The torch symbolizes liberty, while the outer circle of 13 stars stands for the original colonies. The five stars forming the inner semicircle represent the states that joined the Union before Indiana. The large star above the torch stands for Indiana itself. Adopted 1917.

IOWA

Iowa was part of the territory of Louisiana purchased from France by the American government in 1803. This historical link with France is recalled in the state flag. Like the French flag, it is a vertical tricolour of blue, white and red stripes, but has the white stripe twice as wide as the others. The flying eagle has a scroll in its beak that reads 'Our liberties we prize and our rights we will maintain'. Adopted 1921.

KANSAS

One of the flags of Kansas is plain blue with the state seal in the centre above the name of the state. At the top of this flag, adopted in 1963, is a small sunflower, the state flower. Another flag used in the state bears the sunflower alone.

KENTUCKY

The state seal appears on the plain blue flag adopted by Kentucky in 1963. It depicts two men shaking hands, an illustration of the encircling motto 'United we stand, divided we fall'. Above the seal are the words 'Commonwealth of Kentucky' and below, forming a garland, are two flowering stalks of goldenrod, the state flower.

103

LOUISIANA

In the centre of Louisiana's blue flag is an emblem taken from the state seal and representing self-sacrifice and devotion: a pelican wounding herself to feed her young. The scroll bears the words 'Union, Justice & Confidence'. The design first appeared in 1812 but was not officially adopted until 100 years later.

MAINE

Maine's flag has a plain blue field with the state coat-of-arms in the centre. In the white shield is a moose lying beneath a pine tree. The supporters are a farmer holding a scythe and a sailor with an anchor. The crest is the North Star above a scroll bearing the word *Dirigo* (I direct). In the compartment is the name of the state. Adopted 1909.

MARYLAND

The flag flown by Maryland is the heraldic banner of Lord Baltimore who founded the colony in 1632. The flag quarters the arms of the family of Lord Baltimore's father, the Calverts (in the first and fourth quarters) with the arms of his mother's family, the Crosslands (in the second and third quarters). The present design was adopted in 1904.

MASSACHUSETTS

The design of the present flag of Massachusetts dates from 1971. It is a plain white flag with different emblems on the obverse and reverse sides. The obverse has the state arms, a shield charged with a white star and an Indian in yellow. The crest is a raised arm holding a sword. Below is a blue scroll with Latin words meaning 'With the sword she seeks peace under liberty'. The reverse of the flag has a blue shield charged with a green pine tree, the traditional emblem of New England.

MICHIGAN

Adopted in 1911, the flag of Michigan displays the state coat-of-arms on a blue field. The shield contains a scene with the word *Tuebor* (I shall defend) in the chief. The supporters are an elk and a moose; the crest is an eagle. Below is a scroll with the Latin words for 'If you seek a beautiful peninsula, look about you'.

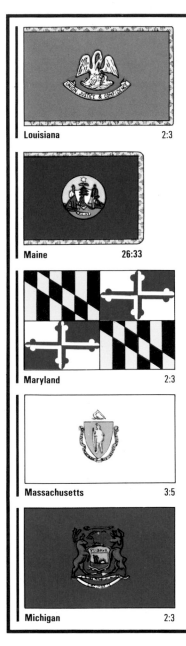

Louisiana   2:3

Maine   26:33

Maryland   2:3

Massachusetts   3:5

Michigan   2:3

Minnesota 3:5

Mississippi 2:3

Missouri 7:12

Montana 3:5

Nebraska 3:5

MINNESOTA
In the centre of Minnesota's blue flag is the state seal. It contains a scene in which a white pioneer farmer watches an Indian horseman riding towards the west, an historical reference to the displacement of the Indians by the westward spread of white settlers. The scroll in the seal and the star-shaped arrangement of stars around the seal are reminders that Minnesota is 'The North Star State'. The present design of the flag dates from 1957.

MISSISSIPPI
The flag of Mississippi, adopted in 1894, refers to the past history of the state. The flag is an adaptation of the 'Stars and Bars' flag flown early in the Civil War by the southern states. It has the southern Battle Flag in the canton and three horizontal stripes in blue, white and red in the field. These are a reference to the French flag and to the time when Mississippi was part of French Louisiana before its purchase by the United States in 1803.

MISSOURI
Three horizontal stripes in red, white and blue in the flag of Missouri recall the time when the state was part of French Louisiana. In the centre of the flag is the state coat-of-arms inside a blue circle containing 24 white stars. The stars indicate that Missouri was the 24th state to join the Union. Adopted 1913.

MONTANA
The flag, adopted in 1905, has a disc in the centre with a view of the Great Falls on the Missouri River. The miners' tools in the foreground, are a reference to the state's mineral wealth. The motto *Oro y Plata* is Spanish for 'Gold and Silver'. The name of the state was added above the disc in 1981.

NEBRASKA
The state seal of Nebraska appears in the centre of the blue state flag adopted in 1925. The scene in the seal depicts a cabin, a steamboat sailing up the Missouri River and a train approaching the Rocky Mountains. In the foreground is a blacksmith at work. The motto is 'Equality before the law'.

NEVADA

Unlike other states that have their state seal on their flags, Nevada displays its seal in the upper hoist. Its design incorporates a central white star encircled by the name of the state inside a wreath of two branches of sagebrush. Above is a scroll bearing the words 'Battle Born', a reference to the fact that Nevada joined the Union during the Civil War. Adopted 1929.

NEW HAMPSHIRE

Introduced in 1909 and slightly changed in 1932, the flag of New Hampshire displays the state seal in the centre of a wreath of laurel sprigs and nine stars. The number of stars indicates that the state was the ninth to join the Union. One of the first ships in the American navy, the frigate *Raleigh*, appears in the central scene.

NEW JERSEY

The buff colour of New Jersey's flag is unique among American state flags. It is said to represent the colour chosen by George Washington for part of the uniform of New Jersey troops in the War of Independence. The flag has the state coat-of-arms in the centre. The shield depicts three ploughs symbolizing agriculture. The supporters are a woman holding the cap of liberty on a pole and another woman carrying a cornucopia. They illustrate the words in the motto: Liberty and Prosperity. Adopted 1896.

NEW MEXICO

The red and yellow colours of New Mexico's flag recall the time when the state belonged to Spain. In the centre of the yellow field is an ancient sun symbol used by the Zuñi Indians living in the state. Adopted 1925.

NEW YORK

The blue flag of New York state, adopted in 1901, has the state coat-of-arms in the centre. The shield depicts two sailing ships on the Hudson River; the supporters are two women symbolizing liberty and justice; the crest is an American eagle perched on a globe turned to show the North Atlantic Ocean. The motto below is simply 'Excelsior'.

NORTH CAROLINA

The colours and stripes in North Carolina's flag recall the 'Stars and Bars' flag used by the southern states early in the Civil War. North Carolina's flag has two equal, horizontal stripes, red over white, with a blue vertical stripe in the hoist. An emblem in the blue stripe displays a white star flanked by the initials of the state in yellow. Above and below are yellow scrolls commemorating important dates in the state's history.

NORTH DAKOTA

North Dakota has two flags, one for general use, illustrated opposite, and another for official state use. The flag illustrated is based on the regimental colours of the 1st North Dakota Infantry, which fought in the Spanish-American War of 1898, and was adopted in 1911.

OHIO

Ohio's flag, adopted in 1902, is striking not only in its design but also in its unique shape, a swallow-tailed pennant. The blue triangle at the hoist bears a red disc edged in white to make a large letter 'O' for Ohio. This circular symbol also refers to Ohio's nickname, 'The Buckeye State'. The 17 white stars indicate that Ohio was the 17th state to join the Union.

OKLAHOMA

In the centre of Oklahoma's light blue flag is a device symbolizing peace between the original Indian people and the white settlers. It consists of an Osage Indian shield upon which an Indian peace pipe is crossed with an olive branch. The present design dates from 1941.

OREGON

The obverse of Oregon's blue flag displays the name of the state at the top and the date of joining the Union, 1859, at the bottom. In the centre is the shield from the state coat-of-arms, with a garland of 33 stars indicating that Oregon was the 33rd state to join the Union. The shield contains a scene symbolizing white settlement on the west coast. The reverse side of the flag bears a gold beaver. Adopted 1925.

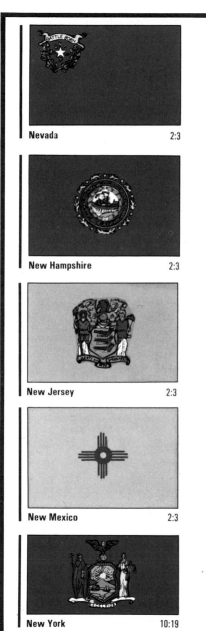

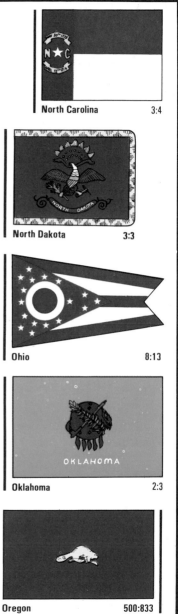

Nevada 2:3

North Carolina 3:4

New Hampshire 2:3

North Dakota 3:3

New Jersey 2:3

Ohio 8:13

New Mexico 2:3

Oklahoma 2:3

New York 10:19

Oregon 500:833

Pennsylvania 27:37

Rhode Island 29:33

South Carolina 2:3

South Dakota 3:5

Tennessee 3:5

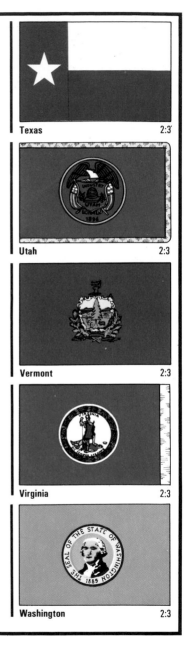

Texas 2:3

Utah 2:3

Vermont 2:3

Virginia 2:3

Washington 2:3

PENNSYLVANIA

The state coat-of-arms appears in the centre of the blue flag Pennsylvania adopted in 1907. The ornate shield depicts a sailing ship, a plough and three wheatsheaves. The supporters are black horses and the crest is an eagle. The red scroll bears the words 'Virtue, Liberty and Independence'.

RHODE ISLAND

The flag of Rhode Island, like that of neighbouring Massachusetts, is white. Placed prominently in the centre is a large gold anchor above a blue scroll bearing the word 'Hope'. This emblem dates from 1647, when Rhode Island was a British colony. The 13 stars around the anchor and scroll stand for the original 13 colonies. The present design dates from 1897.

SOUTH CAROLINA

The flag of South Carolina dates back to a design of 1775 known as the Moultrie flag, an unofficial blue flag with a white crescent in the upper hoist. In 1860 South Carolina became the first state to secede from the Union, and in the following year it adopted the Moultrie flag as its official flag, but with a white palm-tree added in the centre. This design is still the official flag of the state.

SOUTH DAKOTA

Originally adopted in 1909, the design of South Dakota's flag was revised in 1963 so that both sides became identical. In the centre of the flag is the state seal inside a serrated yellow border representing the sun. Around this are the words 'South Dakota, The Sunshine State'. The seal may appear on either a white or light blue background.

TENNESSEE

The flag Tennessee adopted in 1905, has a striking design in the national colours of red, white and blue. The plain red field has a narrow vertical blue stripe, fimbriated in white, in the fly. In the centre is a blue disc, also fimbriated in white, containing three white stars. The stars indicate that Tennessee was the third state to join the Union after the original 13 colonies.

TEXAS

The red, white and blue flag of Texas dates from 1839. It was the flag of the independent Republic of Texas, which had rebelled against Mexican rule in 1835. The design has two horizontal stripes, white over red, in the fly, with a vertical blue stripe containing a white star in the hoist. The flag gave the state its popular name of 'The Lone Star State'.

UTAH

A thin gold ring in the centre of Utah's flag contains the state coat-of-arms. This has two crossed American flags upon which is a blue shield depicting a beehive with the words 'Industry' and 'Utah'. The crest is an eagle. Below the shield are two dates: 1847, when the state was founded by the Mormons and named the 'Land of the Honey Bee', and 1896, when the state joined the Union. Adopted 1911 and redesigned in 1913.

VERMONT

Vermont's blue flag, adopted in 1923, has the state coat-of-arms in the centre. The shield depicts a green landscape in which appears a large pine tree. Beneath the tree are three wheatsheaves and a cow. In the distance is a range of blue mountains. Below, on a red scroll, is the state motto, 'Freedom and Unity'.

VIRGINIA

Virginia was one of the 13 colonies which broke away from Britain in the War of Independence. This is dramatically symbolized in the state seal shown on its flag. Beneath the name 'Virginia' an armed female figure is seen trampling a fallen figure from whose head a crown has fallen. Below is a Latin motto meaning 'So always with tyrants'. The seal dates from 1776, the flag from 1861.

WASHINGTON

Washington is the only state with a green flag. In the centre is the state seal dating from 1889, the year when the state joined the Union. Inside a yellow circle is a portrait head of George Washington, after whom the state was named. Adopted 1923, revised 1967.

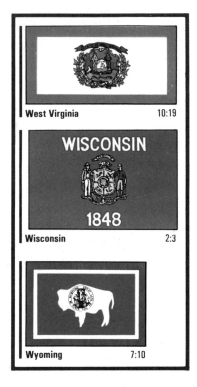

West Virginia   10:19

Wisconsin   2:3

Wyoming   7:10

Bermuda   1:2

Mexico   4:7

WEST VIRGINIA
The blue-bordered white flag of West Virginia, adopted in 1929, displays the state coat-of-arms in the centre. The ornate shield contains figures of a farmer and a miner by a rock inscribed with the date in 1863 when the state joined the Union. The Latin motto means 'Mountaineers always free'.

WISCONSIN
The blue flag bears the state's coat of arms in the centre. This has a shield which is charged with traditional implements from the life of the state. The crest is a badger, since Wisconsin is known as 'The Badger State'. The name of the state above the arms, and the date 1848 below, all in white, were added in 1981.

WYOMING
The blue flag of Wyoming has a double border in red and white. The white silhouette of a buffalo in the centre recalls the time when the state supported great herds of these animals. Within the silhouette is the state seal. Adopted 1917.

Wyoming is the last in the alphabetical list of states in the United States. The flags of other countries in North and Central America are described in the following pages.

BERMUDA
The British dependent territory of Bermuda, off the eastern coast of North America, flies an unusual distinguishing flag. Instead of the customary British Blue Ensign, it is the Red Ensign, with the shield from Bermuda's badge in the fly. The shield depicts a red lion holding another shield in which the shipwreck of the *Sea Venture* in 1609 is depicted.

MEXICO
The national flag of Mexico is a vertical tricolour of green, white and red stripes with the national emblem in the centre. The stripes were inspired by the French tricolour. The emblem of the eagle, snake and cactus is based on an ancient Aztec legend about the founding of Mexico City. The design dates from 1821, the present version from 1968.

Guatemala   5:8

Belize   13:19

Honduras   1:2

El Salvador   3:5

GUATEMALA
Guatemala was one of the five Central American countries that broke away from Spanish rule on 15 September 1821 and formed the United Provinces of Central America. The others were Honduras, El Salvador, Nicaragua and Costa Rica. Their flag consists of 3 horizontal stripes of blue, white and blue, based on the flag of Argentina. It was first flown on an island off Nicaragua in 1818 at the beginning of the struggle for independence. The federation finally split up in 1839, but its flag is still the basis of the national flags flown today by its former members.

Guatemala has changed the United Provinces flag to 3 vertical stripes. The present version dates from 1971. The state flag and naval ensign bears the national arms in the centre. Its design incorporates a quetzal bird perched on a parchment on which is inscribed the date of the country's independence from Spain: 15 September 1821.

See also the descriptions of the flags of Honduras, El Salvador, Nicaragua and Costa Rica.

HONDURAS
The national flag of Honduras is the horizontal blue, white and blue striped flag of the United Provinces of Central America from 1821 (see Guatemala). Honduras left this federation in 1838, but in 1866 added a group of five blue stars to its flag to express a hope for a new federation in the future. The present design was adopted in 1949.

BELIZE
The new flag was adopted on independence in 1981. In the centre is a white disc with the coat of arms surrounded by a garland of leaves. At the top and bottom are red stripes, which were added to the original flag when it was adopted as the flag of independent Belize.

EL SALVADOR
In 1912 El Salvador re-adopted the striped flag of the United Provinces of Central America, which it had first hoisted after breaking away from Spain in 1821 (see Guatemala). Three versions of this flag are used as the state flag: a plain one; one with the national motto 'God, Union, Liberty'; and a third with the state arms in the centre.

Nicaragua   3:5

Costa Rica   3:5

Panama   2:3

NICARAGUA
Except for a slight difference in the shade of the blue, the national flag of Nicaragua is identical to that of neighbouring El Salvador, with its 3 horizontal stripes of blue white and blue. It was adopted by Nicaragua and the four other members of the United Provinces of Central America after they broke away from Spain in 1821 (see Guatemala). The present version of the flag dates from 1971.

An alternative design to that illustrated serves as the national and merchant flag, naval ensign and army flag. It was the same striped design but also displays the triangular state emblem in the white stripe. The design of this emblem also derives from that adopted by the United Provinces. A variation of this emblem can be seen in one of El Salvador's alternative state flags.

COSTA RICA
The national flag of Costa Rica is an interesting example of a design which has evolved in stages over a number of years. The present design, adopted in 1964, has a balancing sequence of horizontal stripes: dark blue, white, red, white, dark blue, with the central red stripe twice as wide as each of the others. In the red stripe, set towards the hoist, is a white oval containing the state arms.

The origin of this flag was the horizontal blue, white and blue stripes of the United Provinces of Central America, a group of five countries including Costa Rica that broke away from Spain in 1821 (see Guatemala). Costa Rica left this federation in 1838 and for a time flew a flag with a different arrangement of stripes: white, blue and

white. In 1848 the present design was adopted.

Although private citizens are not permitted by law to fly the flag illustrated on land, in practice a flag without the state emblem (the merchant flag) is often seen.

PANAMA
The distinctive design of the Panamanian flag was adopted in 1903 shortly after the country broke away from Colombia. The colours of its quarters are symbolic: the blue stands for the conservative party, the red for the liberals, while the white represents a hope for peace between them. The blue star stands for public honesty and virtue, the red star for law and order.

HAITI
A black square at the hoist and a red square in the fly make up the strikingly simple design of Haiti's national flag flown since 1964. It is based on a flag with blue and red vertical stripes adapted from the French tricolour in 1803, at the beginning of the struggle for independence from France. The blue stripe was said to represent the

nation's black people, the red stripe its mulattoes. The white stripe, a symbol of white domination, was omitted. For a brief time in 1806 the blue stripe was changed to black, and this flag was re-adopted as the national flag of Haiti in 1964.

DOMINICAN REPUBLIC
A white cross divides the national flag of the Dominican Republic into quarters of red and blue. The design dates from 1844, when the Dominican people, led by the Trinitarian movement of Pablo Duarte, finally won their independence from both Spain and Haiti. The design was based on the flag of Haiti, which then ruled Dominica. This had horizontal stripes of blue over red. To this flag the Dominicans added a white cross and later reversed the blue and red quarters in the fly.

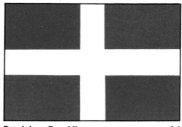

Haiti 1:2

Dominican Republic 2:3

Cayman Islands 1:2

Jamaica 1:2

CAYMAN ISLANDS
As a British dependent territory, the Cayman Islands fly a distinguishing flag comprising the British Blue Ensign with a white roundel in the fly containing the islands' coat-of-arms.

JAMAICA
On independence from Britain in 1962 Jamaica hoisted a national flag of a distinctive design. It has a gold saltire dividing the field into black triangles at the hoist and fly and green triangles at the top and bottom. The gold stands for Jamaica's natural resources and sunshine; the green for its agriculture and hope for the future; and the black for the nation's hardships, both past and present.

CUBA
Cuba's national flag, the 'Lone Star' banner, was designed in 1849 and officially adopted when the island finally gained its independence from Spain in 1902. The blue stripes stand for the three provinces of the island in 1849, while the red triangle represents the Cuban people's bloody struggle for independence.

Cuba 1:2

THE BAHAMAS

To the north-east of Cuba, in the Atlantic Ocean, lie the 700 islands that together make up the Commonwealth of the Bahamas. When the islands gained their independence from Britain in 1973, they hoisted a new national flag in colours that reflect their favoured geographical position. In the fly are three equal, horizontal stripes in aquamarine, gold and aquamarine. The gold represents the beautiful sandy beaches of the islands, while the aquamarine stripes on either side symbolize the blue-green waters of the surrounding ocean. The black triangle in the hoist stands for the unity of the nation as the people exploit the resources of the islands and the sea around them.

TURKS AND CAICOS ISLANDS

This group of islands in the Atlantic Ocean to the north of Haiti is a British dependent territory. The distinguishing flag flown on the islands has the same basic design as the flags flown by other dependent territories: the British Blue Ensign with the shield from the islands' coat-of-arms in the fly. The gold shield depicts, in their natural colours, a queen conch shell, a spiny lobster and, below, a turk's head cactus, all of which are found in the islands.

PUERTO RICO

The present design of the flag of Puerto Rico was adopted in 1952 when the island became the self-governing Commonwealth of Puerto Rico. Because the island is still a dependent territory of the United States, its flag is flown only in association with the American Stars and Stripes and is placed on its left (as seen by the observer).

The colours of the Puerto Rican flag are those of the Stars and Stripes. But the design is almost identical to the flag of Cuba. It dates from 1895, when the people of Puerto Rico were involved, alongside the Cubans, in a struggle for independence from Spain. Five alternating stripes in red and white appear in the fly, while a blue triangle containing a white star occupies the hoist.

BRITISH VIRGIN ISLANDS

To the east of the island of Puerto Rico are the islands that make up the British dependent territory of the Virgin Islands. As their distinguishing flag the islands fly the British Blue Ensign with their badge in the fly. This consists of a green shield on which is a female figure draped in white and wearing sandals, like one of the Vestal Virgins of ancient Greece. In her right hand is an antique oil lamp burning with a red flame. On either side of her are two vertical rows of identical lamps, five on the left (dexter) and six on the right (sinister). Below the shield is a gold scroll bearing the motto *Vigilate* (Be alert).

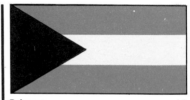

Bahamas   1:2

Turks and Caicos Islands   1:2

Puerto Rico   2:3

VIRGIN ISLANDS OF THE UNITED STATES

As their official name suggests, the Virgin Islands of the United States are an American dependency. The flag illustrated has been flown on the island since 1921. In the centre of the white field is an emblem based on the United States coat-of-arms. It consists of an American eagle with wings outstretched and on its breast a shield containing 13 vertical stripes in red and white beneath the blue chief. The emblem appears between the initial letters of the islands' name, 'V' and 'I', in blue.

ANGUILLA

The status of the Caribbean island of Anguilla is at present in dispute. In 1967 the island was joined to and then seceded from an Associated State of Great Britain comprising the islands of St Christopher, Nevis and Anguilla itself. Since its secession Anguilla has flown its own separate flag, which is not recognized internationally.

Anguilla's unofficial flag has a white field on which appears a group of three interlocking orange dolphins. At the bottom is a narrow blue-green stripe. The white stands for peace; the blue-green stripe for the sea, youthfulness and hope; and the dolphins for strength and endurance. The whole design is said to suggest the aspirations of the newly emergent nation.

ST CHRISTOPHER NEVIS

Commonly known as St Kitts-Nevis, these two islands achieved independence under a new flag in September 1983. The flag was a winning entry in a design competition, and its colours are traditional West Indian. It replaces the flag used since 1967, when St Kitts-Nevis and the island of Anguilla together formed an Associated State of Great Britain. Anguilla seceded from the group, but St Kitts-Nevis retained the old flag, which was a vertical tricolour of green, yellow and blue with a palm tree in the centre. The two stars in the new flag do not represent the two islands, but stand for hope and liberty.

Virgin Islands (U.K. admin)   1:2

Anguilla (Unofficial)   1:2

Virgin Islands (U.S. admin)   2:3

St Christopher Nevis   10:17

ANTIGUA-BARBUDA

Like the nearby islands of St Christopher, Nevis and Anguilla, the Caribbean island of Antigua became a self-governing Associated State of Great Britain in 1967. The striking design of the new flag adopted at that time was chosen out of 600 submitted designs. The flag was divided into three triangular shapes by joining the top of the hoist and the fly to the centre of the foot. The two outer triangles thus form a red field to the design in the central triangle. This contains three unequal, horizontal stripes, black over blue over white. In the black stripe a golden sun rises above the blue stripe

The colours of the flag have a symbolic significance. The red stands for the vigour of the Antiguan people; the blue for hope for the future; the black for the people of the island. The colours in the central triangle – gold, blue and white – also represent the tourist attractions of Antigua: the sunshine, sea and fine beaches. The islands became independent under their new name on 1st November 1981.

MONTSERRAT

As a British dependent territory, the Caribbean island of Montserrat flies the customary British Blue Ensign with the island's distinguishing badge in a white roundel in the fly. This consists of a blue shield with a brown base representing the ground. Rising out of this is a black Passion cross, grasped in the right arm of a female figure in a green robe. Her left hand supports a gold harp resting on the ground in front of her.

DOMINICA

In 1978 the Caribbean island of Dominica gained full independence from Britain and adopted a green flag charged with a broad cross. The arms of the cross are divided into three equal stripes in yellow, black and white, arranged from left to right in the vertical arms and from top to bottom in the horizontal arms. At the centre of the cross is a large red circle containing, in natural colours, a parrot, perched on a brown twig and facing the fly. Round the parrot, within the circle, are ten green stars with yellow borders. In 1981 the black and white parts of the cross were transposed.

ST LUCIA

The Caribbean island of St Lucia became an Associated State of Great Britain in 1967 and adopted a flag with a distinctly modern design. In the plain blue field is a device consisting of superimposed white, black and gold triangles. This is a symbolic representation of St Lucia itself: surrounded by the blue ocean, the black volcanic hills of the island rise up above the sandy beaches.

ST VINCENT AND THE GRENADINES

St Vincent became independent under this name in 1979, and adopted a new flag of blue, yellow, and green. In the centre is a leaf of the breadfruit tree, charged with the whole arms of the state. This flag is based on the winning design in a competition.

BARBADOS

On its independence from Britain in 1966, the island of Barbados hoisted a new flag that indicated both a link and a break with the past. This is suggested by the broken-off head of the trident which appeared in its former colonial badge. The field of the flag is formed by three vertical stripes in blue, gold and blue. The colours represent the island's blue sea and sky and its beautiful golden beaches.

GRENADA

The national flag adopted by the island of Grenada on its independence from Britain in 1974 contains a representation of a nutmeg, the island's chief export. The strikingly colourful design of the flag is divided diagonally into four triangles, yellow at the top and bottom, green in the hoist and fly. Six yellow stars in the broad red border and another in a red disc at the centre of the flag stand for the island's seven parishes.

NETHERLANDS ANTILLES

The six islands that form the self-governing Netherlands Antilles are represented in their flag by six white stars on the horizontal blue stripe in the centre. The field of the flag is white with a vertical red stripe in the centre. The islands adopted the flag in 1959.

Antigua 2:3

St Vincent 4:7

Montserrat 1:2

Barbados 2:3

Dominica 1:2

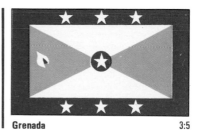

Grenada 3:5

St Lucia 5:8

Netherlands Antilles 2:3

FLAGS OF SOUTH AMERICA

Trinidad & Tobago

Venezuela

Guyana

French Guiana

Surinam

Colombia

Ecuador

Peru

Brazil

Bolivia

Paraguay

Uruguay

Argentina

Chile

Falkland Islands

TRINIDAD AND TOBAGO

Since their independence from Britain in 1962 the islands of Trinidad and Tobago have flown a red flag with a black stripe fimbriated in white running diagonally from the top of the hoist to the foot of the fly. The red is said to stand for the warmth and vitality of the people; the black for their strength and the wealth of the islands; and the white for the sea and the aspirations of the people.

Trinidad & Tobago   3:5

VENEZUELA

The state flag of Venezuela is a horizontal tricolour of equal stripes, yellow over blue over red. In the blue stripe is an arc of seven white five-pointed stars representing the seven provinces that formed the Venezuelan Federation in 1811. In the upper hoist is the state coat-of-arms, its shield depicting a wheatsheaf, representing national unity; a group of weapons standing for victory and independence; and a wild horse, symbolizing liberty.

The colours of the stripes are also seen in the flags of Colombia and Ecuador (see page 120). They are based on the tricolour brought to Venezuela in 1806 by Francisco de Miranda, with the invading liberation army that fought for Venezuelan independence from Spain. The present design dates from 1954.

Venezuela   2:3

GUYANA

When it became independent from Britain in 1966 Guyana hoisted a new flag with a striking triangular design. The colours have symbolic significance. The green stands for Guyana's green land; yellow, its mineral resources; white, the country's many rivers; red, the energy of the people as they build the nation's prosperity; and black, their perseverance in the fulfilment of this task.

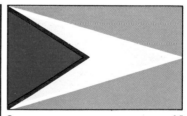

Guyana   3:5

SURINAM

In 1975, after independence from the Netherlands, Surinam adopted a flag with five horizontal stripes in green, white, red, white and green, the red being twice the width of the green and the green twice that of the white. In the central red stripe is a large yellow five-pointed star.

Surinam   2:3

GUYANE (FRENCH GUIANA)

The official flag flown over Guyane is the French tricolour. The territory has been a French possession since 1676, apart from a period of foreign control from 1809 to 1817, and is now an overseas department of France.

BRAZIL

The green flag of Brazil has a central yellow lozenge containing a blue disc representing the night sky seen over Rio de Janeiro (but reversed as in a mirror). Across this disc is a curving white band inscribed with a motto meaning 'Order and Progress'. The green colour symbolizes Brazil's vast forests; the yellow and the diamond shape represent its great mineral wealth.

The design of the flag dates back to a similar flag hoisted in 1822 when the king of Brazil declared his country's independence from Portugal. In 1889 his coat-of-arms was replaced in the centre of the flag by a blue disc with stars, as in the present flag and with the same motto. As the country developed, the number of stars increased from the original 21 to 23. The latest version of the flag was adopted in 1968.

COLOMBIA

The national flag of the Republic of Colombia is a horizontal tricolour of yellow, blue and red stripes. The yellow stripe in the upper half of the flag equals the width of the other two stripes combined.

The colours are almost identical to those of the flags of Venezuela and Ecuador. They were used in the flag created by the patriot Francisco de Miranda in 1806 and flown by Simón Bolívar, whose armies won independence from Spain for Colombia, Venezuela, Ecuador, Peru and Bolivia between 1810 and 1824. The colours were said to represent the golden land of South America (yellow) separated from colonial Spain (red) by the ocean (blue). The design dates from 1861.

ECUADOR

The flag flown by private citizens of Ecuador is almost identical to the national flag of Colombia, the only differences being in the shade of the blue and the proportions of the flag. Ecuador's flag, like those of Colombia and Venezuela, originated in the flag flown by the patriot leader Simón Bolívar early in the 19th century.

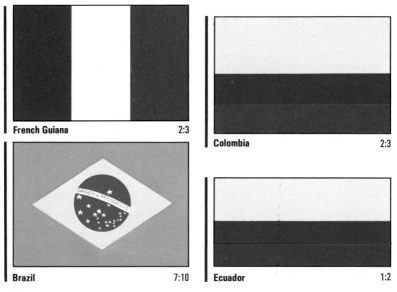

French Guiana   2:3

Colombia   2:3

Brazil   7:10

Ecuador   1:2

Peru 2:3

Paraguay 1:2

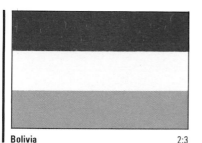

Bolivia 2:3

Uruguay 2:3

PERU

The national flag flown by private citizens of Peru since 1825 is a vertical tricolour of red, white and red stripes. The colours are said to have been chosen by the Argentinian patriot General José de San Martín, who arrived with an army in 1820 to liberate Peru from Spanish rule. He is said to have seen a flock of flamingoes passing over his troops and, taking this as a good omen, to have exclaimed 'Look, the flag of liberty!' The red and white colours of the birds were thus adopted as the flag of his army. (For Peru's state flag see page 21.)

BOLIVIA

Since 1888 the same horizontal tricolour of red, yellow and green stripes has been flown as the national and merchant flag of Bolivia. It was based on an earlier flag adopted in 1851 by the country's first president. The red is said to stand for Bolivia's animals and the valour of its army; the green for its plants and fertile land; and the yellow for its mineral wealth.

PARAGUAY

The national flag of Paraguay is a horizontal tricolour of red, white and blue stripes. In the centre of the obverse is the state emblem, which displays the May Star commemorating Paraguay's liberation from Spanish rule on 14 May 1811. On the reverse, not illustrated, the state seal appears in place of the emblem. It depicts a lion guarding a staff bearing a red cap of liberty. The first version of the flag was hoisted in 1811, the present design in 1842.

URUGUAY

Uruguay has flown the same national flag since 1830, shortly after Britain intervened in a war with Brazil and brought about Uruguay's independence as a separate state. The blue and white stripes and gold sun were derived as early as 1812 from the striped flag and May Sun emblem used in Argentina during the struggle for independence from Spain. The stripes represent the nine provinces of Uruguay at the time of independence in 1828.

CHILE

Designed by an American citizen serving in the Chilean army in 1817, the national flag of Chile was inspired by the American Stars and Stripes. It has two equal, horizontal stripes, white over red, with a blue canton charged with a white five-pointed star. The colours are said to have symbolic significance. The white represents the snow on the peaks of the Andes to the east; the blue symbolizes the clear blue sky above them; and the red stands for the blood of the nation's patriots.

The design was officially adopted in 1817, during the struggle for independence from Spain.

Chile   2:3

ARGENTINA

Above and below the white central stripe of Argentina's national flag are two stripes in a shade of blue known as 'celeste'. This colour, together with white, became a national symbol early in the struggle for Argentina's independence from Spain at the beginning of the 19th century. The two colours were used in a cockade worn by the liberation army and handed out to crowds that gathered in Buenos Aires on 25 May 1810 to demand self-government from the Spanish viceroy. The use of celeste and white as a symbol of revolution then spread to the rest of the country, and in 1812 a military flag in these colours was raised in the city of Rosario. On 9 July 1816, following the lead given by Buenos Aires, the provinces of Argentina also declared their independence from Spain, and just over two weeks later, on 25 July, the celeste and white striped flag officially became the national flag of free Argentina.

The 'May Sun' in the centre of Argentina's state flag flown since 1818 became a national symbol in 1810. It commemorates the appearance of the sun through the clouds as the demonstration to demand self-government gathered in Buenos Aires on 25 May in that year.

Argentina's colours and May Sun also became symbols of Uruguay's struggle for independence from Spain and appear in its flag. The flags of some Central American countries were also influenced by Argentina's flag.

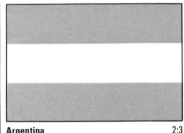

Argentina   2:3

Falkland Islands   1:2

FALKLAND ISLANDS

Together with its dependencies of South Georgia and the South Sandwich Islands, the Falkland Islands are a British dependent territory flying its own distinguishing flag. Its design comprises the British Blue Ensign with a white roundel in the fly containing the islands' badge. This is a blue shield depicting, at the base, a representation of the English ship *Desire*, which discovered the islands in 1592, and, above it, a ram symbolizing the islands' sheep industry. The motto beneath the shield is 'Desire the Right'.

DEPENDENT TERRITORIES
The following territories are dependencies of countries whose flags are shown on the preceeding pages. Some of them have local flags of their own which are only used within the territory. These are marked with an asterisk.

FRANCE
Overseas Departments (reckoned as part of France): Guyane (French Guiana), La Réunion, Martinique, Guadeloupe (with St Barthélemy, St Martin and other islands), Mayotte (parte of Comoros), St Pierre and Miquelon*.

Overseas Territories: Southern and Antarctic Territories, New Caledonia, French Polynesia*, Wallis and Futura*.

AUSTRALIA
External Territories: Australian Antarctic Territory, Cocos (Keeling) Islands, Christmas Island, Norfolk Island*, Heard and Macdonald Islands, Ashmore and Cartier Islands, Coral Sea Islands.

NEW ZEALAND
Territories Overseas: Tokelau, Ross Dependency, Kermadec Islands.

PORTUGAL
Azores*, Madeira*, Macao.

USA
Unincorporated Territories: Johnston Atoll, Midway Islands, Wake Islands*.

SPAIN
Alhucemas, Ceuta*, Chafarinas, Melilla* and Penon de Velez (all in Morocco). The Balearic Islands* and Canary Islands* are integral parts of Spain.

MOROCCO
Western Sahara* (a disputed territory).

DENMARK
Greenland

NORWAY
Svalbard, Jan Mayen, Bouvet Island, Peter I Island, Queen Maud Land.

CHILE
Easter Island (Rapa Nui), Juan Fernandez Islands.

ECUADOR
Galapagos Islands*.

INDIA
Union Territories Overseas: Andaman and Nicobar Islands, Lakshadweep.

ISRAEL
West Bank* (a disputed territory).

Short Bibliography
In addition to the many useful studies on flags found in various books on heraldry, the following illustrated books are specifically concerned with international flags:

E.C.M. Barraclough & W.G. Crampton, *Flags of the World,* Frederick Warne & Co, 1981

W.G. Crampton, *The Observer's Book of Flags,* Frederick Warne & Co, 1978

C.F. Pedersen, *The International Flag Book in Colour,* Blandford Press, 1971

W.S. Smith, *Flags and Arms across the World,* Cassell, 1980

M. Talocci, *Guide to Flags of the World,* Sidgwick and Jackson, 1982

Index

Note: page numbers printed below in *italics* refer to illustrations

ACKNOWLEDGEMENTS

The author and publishers wish to thank Mr Dennis Quinn and Mr Robert Steadman for their generous help in the compilation of this book and the following for supplying photographs:

British Museum 49; Colorsport 37; Mary Evans Picture Library 11 top, 43 top; Michael Holford 26, 40; Alan Hutchinson 51; Italian State Tourist Office 52; Mansell Collection 43 bottom; National Army Museum 27; National Maritime Museum 47; S.A.T.O.U.R.-83; Transport and General Workers Union 35; ZEFA 8, 10, 11 bottom, 23, 30, 31, 78, 97, 118; Roger Clare 38.

Picture research by Jackie Cookson and Penny Warn